Though Bombs May Fall

The extraordinary story of
George Rue, missionary doctor to Korea

Penny Young Sook Kim ✦ Richard A. Schaefer ✦ Charles Mills

Pacific Press® Publishing Association
Nampa, Idaho
Oshawa, Ontario, Canada
www.pacificpress.com

Designed by Dennis Ferree
Cover photo composite by Dennis Ferree

Copyright © 2003 by
Pacific Press® Publishing Association
Printed in United States of America
All Rights Reserved

Additional copies of this book may be purchased at
http://adventistbookcenter.com

Library of Congress Cataloging-in-Publication Data

Kim, Penny Young Sook, 1945-
Though bombs may fall: the extraordinary story of George Rue, missionary
doctor to Korea/Penny Young Sook Kim, Richard Schaefer, Charles Mills.
    p. cm.
ISBN: 0-8163-1963-4
1. Rue, George Henery. 2. Missionaries, Medical—Korea—Biography
I. Mills, Charles, 1950- II. Schaefer, Richard A. III. Title.

R722.32.R835 K54 2003
610.69'5'092—dc21
    [B]   2002042586

03 04 05 06 07 • 5 4 3 2 1

DEDICATION

To my wonderful friend Grace Rue.

To men and women around the world who willingly
give their lives in service to others.

To children without parents and those who love them
as Jesus loves.

God bless you all.

A portion of the proceeds from the sale of this book is being donated
to scholarships at Loma Linda University, where Dr. Rue
recieved his medical training.

About the Authors

PENNY YOUNG SOOK KIM was born and raised in Korea, graduating from the Seoul Sanitarium and Hospital School of Nursing in 1966. She enhanced her education with a one-year midwifery course and moved to the United States in 1967 where she worked as a registered nurse for eight years at the White Memorial Medical Center in Los Angeles, California.

In 1975, she became a businesswoman.

Penny attended Doctor Rue's memorial service in 1993 and decided that his story needed to be told to a wider audience. She determined that future generations of Koreans and individuals around the world would be inspired and motivated by the Rue legacy.

Two of Penny's three children are following their mother's example in the medical field. One is a registered nurse, the other a physician.

Penny lives with her husband in Redlands, California.

RICHARD A. SCHAEFER, a Forest Falls, California, resident, has been employed by Loma Linda University Medical Center for thirty-six years. He is the author of *LEGACY, Daring to Care, the Heritage of Loma Linda University Medical Center.* Presently, he's serving as a historian working on the Center's centennial celebration.

CHARLES MILLS is a full-time author and video producer working from his home in Berkeley Springs, West Virginia. He has written several children's devotionals, the popular *Shadow Creek Ranch* series, the adult devotional *Echoing God's Love,* and several story CDs. Charles came into this world on February 14, 1950, in the Seoul Sanitarium and Hospital guided by the skillful, loving hands of Doctor George Henry Rue.

Acknowledgments

Many thanks to those who have participated in the creation of this tribute to Doctor Rue.

Consultants

Stan Mattson, C.S. Lewis Foundation.

Don A. Roth, representative, General Conference of Seventh-day Adventists.

Stan Sewell, Del E. Webb Memorial Library, Loma Linda University.

Anne Park, businesswoman.

Ralph W. Perrin, DRPH, dean for student affairs, Loma Linda University.

Joon W. Rhee, MD, Ph. D., lifestyle medicine physician and cell physiologist.

Sung Hyun Um, pastor.

Ralph S. Watts, Jr., former director, Adventist Development and Relief Agency.

Eddie and Marie Cho, friends of Grace Rue.

Story Contributors

Grace Rue, RN, wife of George Henry Rue, MD.

George Henry Rue, Jr., MD.

George Haley, missionary, Sam Yuk University, Seoul, Korea.

Mildred L. Watts, RN, first director of the Seoul Sanitarium and Hospital School of Nursing.

Lee Keun Wha, MD, former director, Seoul Sanitarium and Hospital.
Park Hyuk Syuk, MD, obstetrician/gynecologist, retired.
Rena Chung, RN, Doctor Rue's office nurse.
Verna Pak, RN.
Grace Ahn, former director, Seoul Sanitarium and Hospital School of Nursing.

Contributing Writers

Gere P. Friesen
Norman B. Rohrer
Denise Bell

Authors

Penny Young Sook Kim
Richard A. Schaefer
Charles Mills

My Family

Sae Dong, Fred, Karen, and Walter for their ongoing understanding and logistical support. I hope that our concerted efforts will be a blessing and inspiration to many.

Contents

Preface

It's difficult for anyone who hasn't lived and traveled in the orient, particularly in Korea, to appreciate the flavor of its culture and fully understand the determination of its people to wrestle success from tragedy. This amazing tenacity to survive under the most adverse circumstances remains alive and well wherever you find Korean people.

Many years of hardship under Japanese occupation followed by the agony of the Korean War helped solidify Korea's resolve to survive. George Henry Rue, a Seventh-day Adventist missionary doctor, learned to share the dogged determination of his adopted land while serving under the most adverse and heartbreaking circumstances.

The writers of this book pray that the self-sacrificing spirit demonstrated by the individuals found in these pages will inspire a new generation of young people to look beyond themselves and see, through God's eyes, the needs waiting in every corner of the world.

Introduction

This story might never have been told. The work of Doctor George Henry Rue might have lived only in memory except for one important reality: The far-reaching influence and inspiration he fostered cannot be kept silent.

There is no way that Harry and Elizabeth Rue, George's parents, could have known that their son would grow up to serve for thirty-two years as a physician in Korea during that country's most troubling times.

Spread out before me on my office desk here in Redlands, California, are memories put to words—newspaper clippings, articles from my church's magazines, business documents, personal letters, and handwritten notes, all focusing on Korea, the country of my birth. Many contain photographs of George Rue, a medical missionary who came to the "Land of the Morning Calm" in 1929 with his wife, Mae Belle, and their two children. What he, and those who worked by his side, did for my country was straight out of the Bible. They healed the sick, gave comfort to the downtrodden, made disciples, and introduced thousands to the Master Physician. Doctor Rue treated everyone as though he or she were his own child. When it was time to discipline, he disciplined. When it was time to love, he loved.

I can recall days during the war years when I would walk with the women of my village to the community well and carry water back to our homes. I was one of many who washed clothes in the river and, like millions, lived life as it came. It was for people like us that Doctor Rue traveled so far and did so much.

I trained as a nurse in his precious Seoul Sanitarium and Hospital and often wondered what drove this California surgeon to such depths of dedication and perseverance for the people of Korea. Why did he and his wife give up a lucrative medical practice in the United States to carry out surgical procedures on rickety gurneys in dim light with inadequate instruments in poorly heated hospitals? Why did he remain on the job until he was an old man?

This is the story of my boss, my mentor, and my friend. Although he is sleeping in Jesus now, the institutions he built, the work he began, the lives he changed live on as a testimony to his presence among us.

Today's Seventh-day Adventist Korean-Americans continue to feel the influence of Doctor Rue through the effect he had on their parents.

Over the years, my husband and I have watched our children work in the family business, growing up in an uncertain world. I want them to know the story of Doctor George Henry Rue and to be inspired by it. I want the same for you.

Penny Young Sook Kim
Redlands, California
September 2002

Familiar
Darkness

The scalpel slipped cleanly through the patient's flesh leaving a thin but widening gap across his abdomen. Quickly, in precise and steady movements, the surgeon continued to cut deeper and deeper into the opening, revealing intricate layers of skin, muscle, and fat. Blood oozed from severed capillaries and veins, filling the cavity with bright red fluid.

"Suction," the doctor called quietly.

A white-robed nurse lowered a hissing stainless steel probe into the opening. Gurgling sounds filled the small operating room as blood moved through the instrument and traveled unseen along a narrow hose snaking under the table. Other fingers encased in skin-tight gloves pressed sterile sponges attached to long-necked forceps against the flow of body fluids draining from the shimmering walls of the cavity.

The doctor paused while the nurses did their work, admiring the beauty lying open before him—the intricate weave of muscle tissue; the soft, colorful sheen of various organs; the bright plasma oozing over it all. As many times as he'd gazed into the body of a human being, he'd never grown tired of the incredible sight. It didn't matter what color skin encased the collection of veins, arteries, muscles, organs, and fatty tissue, the view was always the same. Time after time the sight had renewed his admiration for the God who had created such universal elegance.

"Blood pressure falling slightly," a heavily accented voice called from the head of the table. "Other vital signs still good."

Doctor George Henry Rue nodded and glanced at the masked man seated by the head of his patient. All he could see were the eyes of the anesthetist staring back at him. The doctor smiled behind his mask. The man's eyes, like those of every other member of the operating team, didn't look the same as his. The lids were gently curved, the openings a bit smaller. But in those unique facial features shone a beautiful blend of acceptance and love. Such differences between him and his coworkers didn't matter because, years ago, he'd chosen to spend his life in the company of those gentle eyes.

"Good," George said. "This shouldn't take much longer. Our friend here will be back in the rice fields before the harvest."

After more probing and careful cutting, a cyst lay exposed in the bright glare of the operating lamp. It seemed to the surgeon to be benign. Further examination in the lab would be needed to confirm that hope. The doctor's skilled hands manipulated the flesh surrounding the growth, searching for unseen evidence of spread. He found none.

"Scalpel," he ordered.

In seconds a shiny blade attached to a short handle arrived with a soft *plat* on his outstretched gloved hand. Bending forward, he moved the instrument to the base of the tumor and started passing it through soft tissue. He had to be careful because other organs rested dangerously close to the site. If his fingers slipped, he could damage the delicate structures pressing in from all sides.

Slowly, carefully, he cut away the fibrous material surrounding the base of the tumor. "Almost there," he stated more to himself than to his team. "Almost there . . ."

The lights blinked out, casting the room in total darkness. George's fingers froze, his scalpel deep in flesh. The hissing of the suction probe stopped in mid gurgle. The quiet banter of the surgery team fell silent. Every sound, save for the soft rhythmic breathing escaping from the sleeping patient's oxygen mask, vanished.

The scuff of shuffling feet broke the silence. A chair leg scraped against the cement floor, and a table covered with neatly arranged instruments rattled slightly. Suddenly, a piercing beam of light cut through the darkness revealing what appeared to be a room filled with statues. "Just stay where you are," he instructed the nurse holding the flashlight, "and direct the beam into the cavity. I'll finish the operation as quickly as I can. Someone go see if you can start the emergency generator. Everyone else go about your business."

"Doctor Rue," a voice called from the doorway. "It's not just the hospital. All of Seoul is dark."

George shook his head slowly as he bent closer to his work. The North Koreans who controlled the energy production for the entire country were, once again, sending an ominous message to their neighbors to the south. "We're in control of your lights," they seemed to be saying. "Soon, we will be in control of you."

The operation continued as the darkness grew deeper across the land; a darkness that surrounded a peace-loving people and that eventually would throw them headlong into the unspeakable horrors of armed conflict. The year was 1948. Feelings throughout the divided country of Korea were running hotter and hotter, pushing two determined ideologies toward the precipice of war.

Later that night, as Doctor Rue walked from the hospital to his home nearby, he paused in the stillness and gazed up at the stars littering the sky. "You'd be proud of me," he said silently to the memory of his father, whose face was clearly visible in his mind's eye. "You taught me to be prepared for anything and not . . . " He paused. "And not take chances with someone else's life."

That particular lesson had been hard learned.

* * * * *

"Dad, Dad!" Eight-year-old George burst into the kitchen of his Washington home almost out of breath. "Something terrible has happened."

Harry Rue looked up from his morning paper, the scent of fried eggs and hot chocolate still lingering in the air. "Really? What?"

The young boy pointed out the door in the direction of the Columbia River. "The boat my friend and I built, the one I showed you yesterday . . . we went down to the dock to sail it and . . . and . . . it's not there. It's gone! I think someone stole it!"

Harry turned a page and scanned the headlines. "It wasn't stolen."

George blinked. "You . . . you know what happened to my boat?"

The boy saw his father fold the paper and rise from his chair. "I'll show you."

When the two arrived at the water's edge, they peered down into its chilly depth. There, almost masked by the murkiness, was the dull outline of the missing vessel.

"Hey," George gasped. "That's it. That's my boat. It sank!" He frowned and turned to his father. "Dad, I built it right, just like the pictures in the magazine. How could it have sunk?"

"Simple," Harry stated, seating himself on the shore. "I drilled holes in the hull. Went down like a rock."

George stood motionless, mouth sagging open. "You . . . *you* sank my boat?"

"Yep."

"But . . . why?"

"Come, sit down beside me," the man invited.

George obeyed, moving as if in a daze. For a long moment the two sat side by side, staring at the spot where the boat had bobbed the day

George Rue as a young boy.

before. "It wasn't safe," Harry said softly. "You made miscalculations. It was top heavy and, if you and your friend had taken it out on the river, the smallest wave would have capsized you." He pointed. "Water's cold. You might have drowned. I didn't have time to explain to you the problems with the design, and I was afraid you wouldn't believe me if I did. I know how much you love sailing. You might have tried to take it out in spite of my warning. So, I sank it." Harry faced his son. "I couldn't let you gamble with someone else's life—or your own." Lack of knowledge, lack of preparation can be dangerous. You can hurt people with what you *don't* know."

14

George sat in silence. He and his friend had worked hard on that little craft. They'd cut and sanded the pieces of wood, applied the sealing agent, and tried to make up for what they didn't understand about the mechanics of boat building with a fancy paint job and vivid imaginations. Now their labors lay at the bottom of the Columbia River, placed there by his own father.

"You could have taught me," the boy asserted, a slight anger in his voice. "You could have shown me what to do."

"And I will. But you were getting ahead of yourself. Never think that you're too skilled or too important to learn. If sinking your boat teaches you that lesson, it was worth it. Someday you'll understand."

George nodded slowly and then sighed. "So, where did I mess up? What was wrong with my boat?"

The man stumbled to his feet. "Tomorrow, we'll go sailing on a vessel that's built right. We'll spend the whole day at it, OK? We'll learn how boats are supposed to be designed so that they can take the waves and not tip over. We'll ask questions and find answers, and we'll do it together, OK?"

True to his word, the very next morning Harry took George out for a day of sailing. The two enjoyed the brilliance of the sunshine and spent time discovering the proper and safe way to build a proper and safe boat.

* * * * *

Such memories always filled George with happiness. And such memories were flooding his thoughts this night as he walked slowly to his home on the outskirts of a darkened city. Seoul, Korea, was far from the sparkling waters of the Columbia River and the comforting presence of his dad.

But as much as he loved his father, he knew the man wasn't perfect. Before George was born, Harry had received an invitation from someone very respected in the Seventh-day Adventist Church; a woman named Ellen G. White. "You need to move to Oakland, California, and work at the Pacific Press Publishing Association," she had told him. The Pacific Press specialized in printing books and pamphlets highlighting spiritual issues. Harry and his young wife, Elizabeth, eagerly accepted the call and quickly settled into their new life.

But the young father, in spite of his good intentions as a hardworking typesetter, had the unfortunate habit of giving away most of his paycheck to those in need. As the years rolled by, Elizabeth began to realize that her husband's generosity was severely depriving their growing family. She also understood that he wasn't about to change his ways.

At long last, the couple separated, leaving behind a broken family and forcing George to move in with his maternal grandmother in nearby Mountain View where the Press had recently relocated.

He eventually went to live with his physician brother in Stella, Washington, and later with his sister in Forest Grove, Oregon. Because he moved about frequently, young George didn't form deep friendships and grew timid, although he was studious and hardworking. He also kept a dream hidden in his heart.

In spite of being timid and uncomfortable around people, he knew he wanted to make a worthwhile contribution to society. His older brother, whom he respected greatly, had graduated from the University of Oregon School of Medicine. George observed his caring ways and became drawn to the practice of medicine as a way to touch others with the love of Jesus.

He carried that unspoken dream to Laurelwood Academy, an Adventist boarding school located in central Oregon. But things didn't go as planned there either. His grandmother, brother, and sister had always doted on him lovingly. Now, even though surrounded by young people his own age, George felt terribly alone and homesick. So, one day, he ran away.

* * * * *

"He what?" Harry Rue gasped into the handset of his office phone.

"He ran away," Harry's daughter responded. "Showed up here last night. Hitchhiked, I guess. What should I do?"

Harry heard the frustration in Marjorie's voice. "I think I know the problem," the man said encouragingly. "Tell George I'm coming over to see him."

That afternoon, a patient father and runaway son spent hours driving through the beautiful Oregon countryside talking about life, responsibilities, and the future.

"Winners don't run away from challenges," Harry said, eyeing his son thoughtfully.

"I don't feel much like a winner," the teenager admitted, watching the trees slip by. "I don't know anyone at the academy. They're all like strangers."

"Strangers are just friends without names," Harry encouraged. "And you don't run away from friends, do you? No. You stay by them come what may. You show them God's love with your words and actions no matter how they treat you." The man smiled. "Besides, maybe there's a certain someone in the girl's dormitory who's missing you right now. Ever thought of that?"

George blushed. "Oh, Dad. No one is missing me, especially in the girl's dorm. They all think I'm a shy, country boy."

"You *are* a shy, country boy," Harry chuckled. "But, what's wrong with that? Shy country boys have grown up to do great things, and so will you. Marjorie says you want to be a doctor like your brother. I think that's great! However, you have to go to school and earn a medical degree before you can hang out your shingle. Just ask your brother."

George sighed. "You're right, Dad. Maybe if I focused on what I want to accomplish with my life instead of getting all nervous about whether people like me, I could make it at school."

Later that day, George found himself back on the campus of Laurelwood Academy where the father/son outing just "happened" to end. By then a new determination was filling the young man's heart. Over time he made the necessary adjustments, quickly discovering in the process that his dad had been right about friendship.

He found work at a local saw mill and earned enough money to pay his entire tuition through the tenth grade. His grades climbed quickly, and he remained at the top of his class.

George transferred to the Pacific Union College preparatory school in Angwin, California, for his junior year and graduated in 1918. Always resourceful and practical, he found work in the fruit orchards of the Santa Clara Valley picking cherries, prunes, and apricots.

To advance his dream, he enrolled in the two-year premedical course at the college. While carrying a full academic load, he worked forty hours a week cutting and splitting firewood, milking cows, and harnessing the institution's work horses. During the summer, he served as a pipe-fitter's assistant in the shipyards of Vancouver, Washington; a skill that would prove invaluable to him later in a very surprising way in a very unusual place.

* * * * *

Doctor Rue grinned as he glanced back in the direction of the hospital. In his mind's eye he could see the web of pipes running throughout the building, carrying hot water from the boilers in the basement to the radiators in every patient room, office, and surgery. Even now, with the power cut by unfeeling forces to the north, he knew that everyone inside his little hospital was warm and safe, thanks to the skills he'd honed at a faraway shipyard.

He let his gaze drift in the direction of Seoul. The familiar glow in the sky that marked the presence of the city was absent. The doctor shook his head slowly from side to side. What would become of his adopted land? Could it survive yet another war? He shivered in the darkness, knowing full well the unspeakable evil that an armed conflict could bring to a peace-loving people. He knew because he'd been there just a few years earlier when death had first walked in darkness across the land of the morning calm.

The Unspoken Dream

The battered Model T Ford rattled, jerked, bumped twice, and then let loose with a small explosion, leaving three young men sitting in a blue cloud of smoke. "Something's wrong with the engine," one announced.

"You *think?*" George Rue gasped mockingly as he attempted to wave the noxious smoke from his face.

"What do we do now?" the third member of the group asked. "We're medical students, not mechanics. If this bucket of bolts had a broken arm or impacted colon, I could do something about it. But none of my professors have taught me one thing about treating an exploding Ford."

George climbed out from behind the big, round steering wheel and walked to the front of the hissing vehicle. Puffs of steam drifted from under the hood like signal fires from an Indian village. He glanced out across the broad meadows of central California and searched the distant mountains that formed the horizon running north and south. "We need a farmer."

"A farmer?" his friends chorused. "We're trying to drive from Loma Linda to Angwin to see our sweethearts, not plant a crop."

George chuckled. "Farmers know about machinery. They've got tractors and trucks scattered all over the barnyard. I'm sure a farmer could fix our car in nothing flat."

"Don't say the word *flat* in front of this vibrating monster," a companion warned. "We don't want it to get any *new* ideas."

George pointed. "There, beside that stand of trees. I see a house and barn." His two companions joined him and squinted through the warm, spring haze.

"I'll go," one said. "You guys sit tight." He began walking. "And don't eat all the food. Finding Ford-fixing farmers makes me hungry."

George and the remaining classmate dropped down onto the running board of the vehicle and watched as their friend disappeared around a dusty bend in the road. They sat in silence for a long moment until George's companion broke the afternoon stillness. "So, future Doctor Rue, tell me about this woman whom you may or may not get to see this weekend in Angwin."

"Miss Mae Belle Ames." George breathed each word as if speaking of a member of royalty. "She's from Lincoln, Nebraska. Met her while I was at PUC." He grinned broadly. "We're engaged."

"Engaged? So, what are you doing in Southern California while she's 400 miles away in the central part of the state?"

George frowned. "Being very lonely. But, I've got to get my medical degree before I can start a home." The young man leaned in the direction of his friend. "I got kicked out of school because of her," he whispered.

"You did? What happened?"

"Seems the PUC big wigs got wind of our romance and forbade us from seeing each other. I kind of forgot that particular order and, well, ended up working at the naval shipyard on Mare Island for a while waiting for everything to cool down. Helped build the battleship *California*! She's a beauty." George sighed. "Let's just say I'm not held in the highest esteem on the campus of Pacific Union College.

"Oh, and I almost got drafted into the army about that time, too. Received my notice and everything. Like any fine, upstanding citizen, I presented myself at the induction center right on schedule. The sergeant behind the desk suggested I go eat lunch and come back later. I thought he was nuts. However, when I returned, he told me that World War I had just ended and that I could go home." George grinned. "What a nice sergeant."

"Wow!" his companion gasped. "In a few months you got engaged, got kicked out of school, built a battleship, and missed being in the army by one lunch. Life at the medical school must be downright boring for you."

"Lonely. It's very lonely because I miss my Mickey." George blushed. "That's the pet name I gave her. Mickey."

"Oh brother! You really have fallen off the deep end."

"Yes I have, and I'm glad! I've just got to get through medical school so I can marry her. She said she'd wait for me."

"Sounds like she's fallen off the deep end too."

George watched a hawk glide silently through the bright sky. Then he dug the toe of his shoe into the surface of the dusty road. "There's something more . . . something I've got to tell my wife-to-be. Remember when that missionary from Africa spoke to us medical students a few weeks ago at chapel?"

"You mean W. H. Anderson?"

"Yeah. He's a really nice guy. Anyway, I decided something after I heard him speak. You see, I'd been planning to be a family doctor and settle down somewhere with my wife, raise a family, become a pillar of the community, you know, all that good, upstanding doctor stuff. Well, I've changed my mind."

"You've decided *not* to be a good, upstanding doctor?"

"No! I'm going to be a medical missionary . . . in Africa."

"Africa? Are you sure?"

"Yep. More than anything. I mean, think about it; strange new land, new people, a whole new culture, and there I am right in the middle of it, setting broken bones, taking out tumors, diagnosing diseases, saving lives left and right. Doesn't that sound exciting to you?"

His companion laughed. "Hey, you don't have to convince me. But, you might have to do a pretty good sales job on Miss Lincoln Nebraska. She might have other plans for the two of you; something a little less . . . exciting."

George nodded and kicked the tire of the tired Model T. "I know. That's why I was going up to see her this weekend; to talk to her about my dream. Looks like I might not make it."

Just then a voice called from across the furrowed rows of a nearby field. "Hey fellows, meet our very own, made-to-order farmer mechanic.

Says he can fix anything." Behind the smiling medical student walked an older man dressed in coveralls and muddy boots. The new arrival ambled up to the car, took one look at the still-smoldering engine, and shook his head. "This may take a while," he announced.

It did. The farmer and his three unexpected visitors labored over the engine most of that night, surrounded by a barnyard of clacking chickens, barking dogs, and sulking cats. Just as the sun began to peek above the Sierra Nevada Mountains to the east, the engine sputtered to life, and three thankful medical students continued their journey northward.

They rattled onto the campus of Pacific Union College with enough time to visit their sweethearts for just one hour. Then, reluctantly, they climbed on board their temperamental Model T and headed back toward Southern California. The missionary discussion would have to wait for another time, another place.

After completing his freshman year in medical school, George realized that he just couldn't endure another minute of separation from the girl with the soft, wavy, brown hair and loving eyes. So, during the 1921 summer break from classes, George Rue and Mae Belle Ames joined their lives for better and for worse and returned to Loma Linda to set up housekeeping.

Their first child, Betty, arrived red-faced and wailing at White Memorial Hospital in 1923 while George was getting his clinical education in Los Angeles. Strapped for cash, Mickey occasionally sold pints of her own blood to buy her husband special gifts.

All their hard work and sacrifice paid off. George Rue graduated from the College of Medical Evangelists in 1924 at the top of his class! His march down the aisle was followed by an internship at Los Angeles County General Hospital, where, because of his impressive scholastic achievements, he received first choice of the medical services.

The young intern turned down an unsolicited offer to become a surgical fellow at the prestigious Mayo Clinic in Rochester, Minnesota, an offer most physicians would have proudly accepted. Why? Because he and Mickey had a very different future in mind.

George had finally found time to explain his dream of being a medical missionary in Africa and, much to his relief, his adoring wife had agreed wholeheartedly. So, instead of applications going to distinguished hospitals across the country, two neatly typed applications for mission service appeared at the General Conference headquarters of the Seventh-day Adventist Church in Takoma Park, Maryland. Under the "where" column, both Mickey and George wrote in firm, dark letters, "Africa."

George's document contained other pertinent information. Age: 25 years. Weight: 148 pounds. Height: 5'8". Experience: limited experience in mechanics, plumbing, and carpentry. Considerable experience in farming.

Mickey's application reported: Age: 24. Weight: 110 pounds. Height: 5'2". Experience: Stenographer, bookkeeping.

Dr. Percy Magan, dean of the Los Angeles division of the College of Medical Evangelists and close friend and mentor to the young couple, offered a personal recommendation. "Rue is a fine boy and his wife an excellent little woman," he wrote to the General Conference. "They are godly and devoted. I believe you'll like them both."

But, there was one obstacle standing between the young couple and their dream of mission service. The new "Doctor Rue" wanted to retire his medical school debts as soon as possible, so while they waited for an opening somewhere in the mission field, George moved his little family to Calistoga, California, a small resort town guarding the far end of the famous Napa Valley wine country. Here he looked after the practice of a physician who was out of town for several months.

The valley, with its mild climate, clean air, and inspiring scenery would have been a perfect place to settle down, raise a family, and enjoy the good life. When the traveling physician returned, the two doctors worked together for a year.

Then, because of insufficient patient load to keep two practitioners busy, George established a family practice in Kennewick, Washington, a farming and dairy town of about 1,800 inhabitants, situated in the southeastern part of the state.

The nearest hospital stood across the Columbia River in Pasco. It boasted two surgery rooms, a well-equipped delivery room, and fifty beds. It was also a training school, and Doctor Rue accepted the institution's invitation to teach anatomy and physiology to eager, young students.

Unfortunately, the move to Kennewick took place just as the local economy suffered from an economic depression due to a severe winter frost. In order to keep reducing school debts, George and Mickey skimped on meals, postponed the purchase of new clothing, and decided not to replace their aging automobile. In spite of the challenges, Doctor Rue's practice flourished. Mickey, insisting that she, too, make an impact on the community, became an officer in the local thirty-member Seventh-day Adventist church.

Through all the changes and challenges, the young couple maintained their commitment to future medical missionary service. "We want to serve Christ in lands less fortunate, where there's poverty and disease, where God can use us to His glory," they told their church family.

Then, one day, a letter arrived that would change George's and Mickey's lives in a very unexpected way.

George burst into the kitchen clutching an opened envelope in his hand. "You're not going to believe this!" he called to his wife standing elbow deep in dishwashing suds.

Mickey turned to face her husband. "Believe what?" she asked, rinsing soap from her arms.

"Let me read you this letter." As the two seated themselves at the kitchen table, George unfolded a two-page message neatly typed and signed by their friend Dr. Percy Magan. George cleared his throat. "My Dear George and Wife." He paused. "That's us."

Mickey nodded.

"Only recently have I learned that you have moved away from Calistoga and gone up into the great Northwest . . . blah, blah, blah …blah, blah, blah." George glanced up at his wife. "I'll read you the "blah, blah" part later."

"OK."

"Here's the good part." George straightened himself and began again, this time slowly, savoring every word. "There is a wonderful opening for someone in Korea." He glanced over at his wife. "Korea," he whispered. Then he continued reading. "We own a fine twenty-bed hospital in Soonan, beautifully equipped with a good X-ray plant and a nurse and three foreign families already living there. The climate is good, and there are plenty of fruits and vegetables and a nice home for the doctor. This place has been waiting and waiting and waiting for someone to go there for a long, long time until the poor souls are almost discouraged. I wonder if God would not put it into your good hearts to respond to this call."

George refolded the letter and slipped it gently back into its envelope. They'd been dreaming of Africa for so long. They'd pictured themselves at jungle clinics or walking the streets of one of that continent's modern cities doing God's work. Now they were being called to a relatively small country about which they knew nothing.

Slowly, George allowed his gaze to drift to his wife's face. What he saw vanquished any uncertainty he'd been feeling about what her response might be. Mickey wore a gentle smile . . . and a tear. "Looks like God is talking to us," she said.

George nodded slowly. "It certainly does."

"Just one problem," Mickey said, a suddenly somber tone darkening her voice.

"What?"

"It's just that . . ."

"Yes?"

"It's just that . . . I have no idea where Korea is. Do you?"

George's worried frown turned into a relieved grin. "Only one way to find out," he declared, jumping to his feet and taking hold of his wife's hand.

The excited couple hurried over to the bookcase in the living room and retrieved the K volume of the encyclopedia. In minutes they sat head to head, looking at a foldout map populated with islands and land masses sporting strange, exotic titles such as Taiwan, Philippines, Vietnam, China, Ryukyu Islands, Mongolia, Siam. They spoke the names slowly, methodically, enjoying the mysterious sounds that tickled their tongues. Their eager fingers traced the outline of the island of Japan and then, together, moved west across the Sea of Japan to where a peninsula of land jutted south from the mainland of China. There, resting among a small collection of islands and surrounded on three sides by deep waters, lay the country called Korea.

George and Mickey sat for a long moment, gazing down at the map. Each heard the other sigh.

There still remained a familiar obstacle between the couple and their acceptance of this surprise mission call. Money. Being a conscientious medical practitioner, George had purchased the necessary instruments and equipment to meet the demands of his ailing clientele. And there were his school bill obligations as well. In time, he knew he'd be able to pay back all his debts. But, the way things were going, that would take years. Korea needed someone right away; not next year, not two years into the future. Korea needed help *now*. George understood that the only way to free himself from his obligations was to find another doctor who'd buy his growing practice outright.

Days later, as if in response to his prayers, a competitor stopped by the office proposing to George that they join forces to establish a larger clinic. The offer turned into an opportunity to sell his practice, retire his debts, and have spare funds available to step out in obedience to the call they'd received through Dr. Magan.

As soon as George wired the good news to his friend, the General Conference Missions Board stepped in and began guiding the young couple's leap of faith into foreign service, even offering suggestions of what they should pack for their journey to Korea. "Take considerable household effects," they instructed, "second-hand preferably which can enter the country duty free. Bring shoes, socks, and underwear—especially women's underwear. Certain kinds of reasonably priced cloth will be available for someone who can sew."

At long last, early in 1929, after the boxes were packed and tearful goodbyes spoken, George, Mickey, six-year-old Betty, and four-year-old son, George, Jr., stood on a dock in the port of San Francisco gazing up at the huge steamer that would take them out to sea. The vessel, bound for Japan, bore the name SS *Siberia Maru*.

Faces glowing with anticipation, the little family climbed the gangplank and soon watched the coastline of the United States drop from view. Their great adventure had begun. True, it wasn't Africa, but it was an adventure all the same.

Morning Calm

The SS *Siberia Maru* plowed through the swells of the Pacific Ocean for an entire month, carrying the Rue family ever westward, closer and closer to their new life. The vessel's bow pointed to sunset after glorious sunset as it sliced through the waters, leaving behind a shimmering wake that stretched for miles.

To pass the time, George tried his best to prepare his children for what lay ahead.

"It says here that Korea is called 'The Land of the Morning Calm,'" George announced as Betty and George, Jr. crowded around him and the book he was reading. "It has temples and shrines, even an extinct nine-thousand-foot volcano."

"Does it have ice cream?" Betty asked, squirming her way onto her father's lap, quickly followed by George, Jr.

"Well, I don't know. Maybe. It says the people in Korea eat spicy, salty foods and something called kimchi. I wonder what kimchi is? It says it's Korea's best-known delicacy, high in vitamins and nutrients." The doctor frowned. "Oh, this is interesting. They ferment it by burying it in the ground."

"They bury food in the ground?" Betty giggled.

"Yep. And do you know how the Koreans greet each other?"

"No."

"Instead of saying 'Hello,' they say, 'Have you had rice today?' Isn't that neat?"

George, Jr. shook his head. "But what about ice cream?"

"You too?" George laughed. "Now remember, this isn't America. They do things a lot different in Korea than they do in Kennewick. But I know you're going to like it there even if they don't have ice cream. This book says Korea does have ten rivers, lots of high mountains, sandy beaches, and about eight thousand islands. Sounds like a fun place to explore!"

The children agreed that their future home offered a few interesting features, but they felt that a lack of ice cream would definitely represent a negative mark against it as a nation.

Because the Japanese Empire ruled Korea at that time, the Rues were forced to stop in Japan to process their passports. Dr. Getzlaff, director of the Seventh-day Adventist-owned-and-operated Tokyo Sanitarium and Hospital, and his wife met the little family in Tokyo and offered good food, restful sleep, and heartfelt prayers before the journey continued.

On May 7, 1929, the SS *Siberia Maru* cut power and drifted into a strange and fascinating harbor on the western coast of Korea. Even before the features and faces of the land came into sharp focus, the smell of smoldering cooking fires, fermenting kimchi, open sewers, and livestock waste drifted in the still air.

Looking up at the Rues from the bottom of the gangplank stood Ralph and Mildred Watts, Americans who had preceded the Rues to Korea. It was Ralph, in his capacity as home missionary and missionary volunteer secretary for the Korean Union Mission, who had sent the urgent appeal for an American doctor to oversee the hospital in Soonan. His wife, a registered nurse, had kept the facility open and running, but a more permanent solution to the growing needs of the people was imperative. The answer to his plea now gazed down at him from the ship's railing.

With happy hearts the group of American missionaries crowded into Ralph's car and drove to Soonan, a small town of about two thousand on the Yellow Sea near the ancient city of Pyongyang.

"Well, here we are," Ralph enthused as the vehicle pulled up in front of an old, somewhat decaying structure that, at one time, might have been a pretty nice building. Whatever grand visions George had of his future workplace were quickly dashed. Instead of a well-established facility like the Tokyo hospital he'd seen days before, the building before him was what any real estate agent in far away Kennewick would definitely call a "fixer-upper."

"Needs a little paint," Ralph admitted, stepping over a large crack snaking across the cement landing, "and some timbers, a few cement blocks, an odd brick here and there. You might want to put a new floor in the lobby. Oh, and don't try to plug anything in. No electricity, although we do have a pretty reliable generator."

George chuckled in disbelief. "The next thing you'll be telling me is that there's no running water."

"There's no running water."

The young doctor's shoulders sagged. Then, he saw them, a handful of patients, waiting quietly in the hallway, slumped over old, bent, wooden chairs, looking back at him through eyes clouded with pain and uncertainty.

"Just tell me one thing," George said with a sigh. "Why does Soonan smell so . . . so . . . bad?"

Ralph grinned. "It's not Soonan."

"It's not?"

"Nope. It's Korea." Ralph drew in a deep breath and beat his chest as if he'd inhaled the first pure air in weeks. "Welcome home, Doctor Rue." Ralph then proceeded to serve Dr. Rue *bo-ri-ch'a*, a Korean toasted-barley tea.

* * * * *

George stood in the darkness as memories continued to flood his thoughts. He felt tired, but it was a good tired, a weariness that comes only from spending many hours in service to others. Soonan seemed like a very long time ago.

The physician walked a few paces and settled himself on a low retaining wall where the road that curved in front of the Seoul Sanitarium and Hospital intersected the driveway leading to his house. The soft wind blowing in from the north carried with it a chill, the kind that ignores overcoats and sneaks uninvited to the skin. But even as his body shivered, his heart was warmed by visions from long ago.

Glancing down at his hands, he grinned broadly. Fingers that had been trained to search for disease and explore the inner structure of the human body had found additional outlets for service during those first few months on the job.

Soonan Clinic and Hospital Staff, 1939.

This man is being brought to Soonan Clinic and Hospital in style. Most patients were carried by relatives or friends on their backs.

* * * * *

The liberal use of mops, brooms, and paintbrushes, motivated by strong resolve, transformed the Soonan Dispensary and Hospital into a well-groomed facility. Soon it proudly offered rooms for eighteen adults and eight children. Several weeks after his arrival, George wrote to his family in America, "I believe when we are through, we'll have one of the best if not the best-equipped small hospitals in Korea."

The new doctor and his dedicated team of caregivers even created a portable clinic and ventured into surrounding towns to care for the sick. Through such interaction with the Korean people, the Rue family became familiar with their culture, dietary habits, and sometimes-strange customs.

In many cases, what they discovered nearly broke their hearts. The desperately poor, unable to pay for medical services, waited until they were nearly dead before they sought help. George tried to keep the expense of medical attention as low as possible. A hospital bed cost a patient only one Japanese yen a day; about a half-dollar. An appendectomy was billed at fifteen to twenty-five yen; a tonsillectomy, five yen. But even at these incredibly low prices, many in the surrounding area still couldn't afford the luxury of health care. And many were too proud to accept help for which they could not pay.

The clinic treated between twenty and fifty patients a day, many diagnosed with typhoid and dysentery. "On every hand we see poverty and sickness," George wrote to his friend Dr. Magan. "There is much to be done for these people."

In spite of the sacrifices, George and Mickey enjoyed good living conditions. They grew fresh vegetables in their own garden that summer and learned to appreciate and savor the taste of ever-present and ever-essential rice.

Colleagues included one Korean physician, three Korean nurses, and Mrs. Watts. Doctor Rue appreciated the exceptionally competent Mrs. Watts who, besides her regular nursing duties, faithfully administered anesthesia and performed laboratory tests.

Within three months, the newly renovated Soonan Adventist Hospital obtained government approval, enabling it to function as a fully authorized medical facility. Word spread quickly. Patients walked as far as sixty miles to receive treatment, many bypassing the large, well-equipped Christian hospital in Pyongyang. They'd heard about the special care offered by the Yankee doctor and his small but dedicated staff.

The church that had sent the Rues to the mission field did their part as well. Seventh-day Adventists in North America earmarked part of their Thirteenth Sabbath overflow offering for support of the work in Soonan.

For months, Doctor Rue studied the Korean language and fully immersed himself in the customs of the people. Much of what he discovered about the history of his adopted land troubled him greatly.

In 1910, Japan had overrun Korea with military might. The country was no longer a "protectorate" of Japan, but one of its possessions. Mail sent to the peninsula's largest city was addressed to "Seoul, Chosen, Japan." The conquering nation turned the peace-loving land into a rice bowl, exporting most of its bounty, leaving the Koreans hungry. Many farmers were forced to forage for roots, bark, and edible weeds during the winter months. Individual liberties didn't exist. There was no freedom of the press, speech, assembly, or association.

Little love was lost between the two peoples; Japanese considered the Koreans inferior and deserving of discrimination and ridicule. Koreans considered the Japanese barbarians. Uprisings had tried to dislodge the foreign grip, but much bloodshed and harsher conditions were the payback.

One morning, soon after his arrival, George walked into the living room of his friend Ralph and found him sitting on the floor, rocking back and forth, reading his Korean Bible out loud.

"What are you doing?" he gasped.

Ralph smiled. "Having my morning devotions, Korean style."

George sat down beside his friend. "You speak Korean?"

"Sure. You should too."

"I have a hard enough time with English."

Ralph chuckled. "I know a good teacher. He'll have you rattling off Korean words in no time. Besides, think how much better you'll be able to communicate with your patients. They can tell you exactly where it hurts."

George nodded. "Maybe, but I do all right with an interpreter. I don't have a lot of time to accomplish anything except examine and treat patients. But, right now, that's the least of my worries."

"Oh? What's up?"

"As you know, in order to practice medicine here in Korea, I have to pass an extensive series of licensure examinations in Japan. You take one test, wait for the results, then take another. This goes on for weeks! Well, my last exam is next week."

"You'll do fine. Just keep in mind everything you've ever learned and be ready to share it with a bunch of Japanese with stethoscopes."

"I feel totally unprepared. The last exam is on the eye and its various disorders. I've got this medical book that I've been studying like crazy, memorizing every picture. I just hope I know enough to pass."

"Didn't I hear Mickey say that you've got one of those—what do they call it—photographic memories?"

George nodded. "Well, yes. But I've got to have the right photographs in my head for it to work effectively."

Ralph put his hand on his friend's shoulder. "Don't worry, George. God will be with you, and He knows all the right pictures."

When the day for the final exam arrived, George stood in a large hospital in Tokyo surrounded by twenty patients, each with a different eye disorder. The examiner pointed to one of the patients and demanded, "What's the matter with this man's eye?"

George closely studied the badly swollen and discolored face while sending a silent prayer heavenward. Sure enough, a picture he'd seen in his medical book appeared in his thoughts. The young doctor turned to the instructor and outlined not only the problem but the correct treatment as well.

One by one, each patient was reviewed, and, one by one, George was able to correctly identify the problem. He passed the exam with high scores and, eventually, received a license to practice medicine anywhere in the Japanese Empire.

Because young Doctor Rue wanted to make a favorable impression on his Korean patients, he was strict with himself and his staff, requiring nurses to wear shoes while working in the hospital even though wearing shoes indoors wasn't the custom of the country. Nor did he allow the medical staff to carry food in front of patients or eat where they could be seen.

George always presented himself appropriately with a neat, clean gown and short haircut. He wanted his crew to do everything they could do, both in words and actions, to maintain their dignity so that they would be trusted and respected by their patients.

Often Doctor Rue ate at his desk, but he usually skipped meals in order to attend to the many emergencies throughout the wards. This unhealthful practice, along with long hours on the job, soon backfired with deadly force.

"George, you don't look very good," Mickey told him one morning, a year after the family had arrived. "I think you're losing weight again. You're skinny enough as it is! You can't afford to drop another pound."

George nodded, sitting on the edge of the bed holding his midsection, his face pale. "It's my kidneys. I think I've got a real problem. The X-rays I had them take yesterday show stones in both. Another has dropped into my left ureter. This is getting serious." He rose stiffly and tried to stand straight, an action that increased the pain. "I've scheduled a cystoscopic procedure with a kidney specialist in Seoul. But, I don't know what to do. If I leave, they'll close the hospital. But if I go untreated, I could . . . "

"You're no good to anyone dead," Mickey said softly. "We've got to get you fixed up. Let's see what the specialist has to say, then we'll make a decision, OK?"

"OK," George agreed.

After the cystoscopic examination was performed the outlook was dim. "You have a good chance of losing your left kidney," the specialist announced, reading from a report on his desk. "You need medical assistance, and you need it right away."

"I understand," George responded with a weary nod.

Deciding that he wanted to be treated back home in America, George herded his little family aboard the USS *American Mail Line* and sailed east. By the time they arrived in San Francisco, he'd lost even more weight and appeared dangerously wasted.

On October 8, 1930, Dr. Magan sent a telegram to the General Conference and reported, "Doctor George Rue here from Korea with serious case of stones in kidneys and ureter. STOP. Serious operation necessary. STOP. Lost twenty pounds and looks bad but courage good. STOP. Will do all possible."

The difficult and dangerous surgery, performed by Dr. Vern Hunt at White Memorial Hospital in Los Angeles, California, turned the tide. By spring, the attending physicians managed to reverse George's physical decline and even put some weight back on their patient. His complexion grew rosy, and his strength slowly returned.

But another injury was proving harder to treat. George had left his work in Korea undone. From his bed each evening, he could see the setting sun lighting the western sky, and he knew that if he were to follow that glowing orb, he'd find it dawning on a far-away country filled with smiling faces and many, many people in pain. He was needed in Korea, and with each sunset his determination grew. As soon as possible, he'd return.

This time, he'd work within an even bigger field of service. When he reopened his missionary medical practice, it wouldn't be in the small town of Soonan. Now he had his sights set on Seoul!

Permanent Home

"There. Right there." George bent low over the map spread across the dining room table, his finger jabbing at a section of land located just north of the city of Seoul. "It has a good road, nice country atmosphere, and the mission offices are nearby."

Mickey joined her husband and studied the lines and symbols running randomly across the surface of the paper. "How much?" she asked.

"Four hundred dollars an acre."

"How many acres?"

"Twenty."

The woman blinked. "And just where are you going to find eight thousand dollars to buy a piece of Korea?"

George rose to his feet. "No, Mickey. It's not just a piece of Korea. It's . . . it's . . . " Doctor Rue paused to reorganize his thoughts. "Look, we've been here in Seoul for a couple of years now. I've established a clinic while helping to keep things running up in Soonan. But the traveling back and forth is killing me. I spend hours and hours each week on the train that I could spend seeing patients.

"And the work is growing so fast I can hardly keep up. We outgrew our first clinic in that old pottery factory above the Bank of Korea in no time flat. Even the building we're in now accommodates only ten in-patients at a time. But," he pointed down at the map, "on that plot of land I could build a permanent hospital, a home for the medical work in Korea. Don't you see? No more moving from place to place. No more temporary facilities that need fixing up or altering in some way. We'll have our own hospital with a modern operating room, examining rooms, comfortable places for patients to stay, good equipment, and . . . " he motioned for Mickey to join him at the map, "right there, just to the left of that mark. Do you know what that is?"

Mickey bent low and squinted. "A . . . rice paddy?"

George laughed. "Well maybe that's what it is right now, but, someday that's going to be our home! See, we'll have a permanent place to live, too. No more renting apart-

ments or using the homes of fur-loughed missionaries from other denominations. Right there, beside the new Seventh-day Adventist hospital, will be the home of George and Mickey Rue and family. As for traveling to work? Maybe two minutes if I don't walk fast." The man sighed. "That's it. That's my dream."

Mickey slipped her arms around her husband. "It sounds wonderful, George. I like your dream. I really do."

Doctor Rue planted a kiss on

Dr. George and Mrs. Mickey Rue, 1936.

the soft cheek of his beaming wife. "Do you ever wish we'd stayed in America after my illness? Did you really want to come back to Korea, or were you just being a faithful missionary wife?"

"Both," Mickey whispered. "I love Korea. And, I love being a faithful missionary wife, too."

"Good," George said with a smile. "I'm going to take this map over to the mission headquarters and tell the powers that be why they need to spend a lot of money. I just hope they're half as receptive to the idea as you are."

Mickey watched her husband retrieve the paper from the table and head for the door. She smiled. If anyone could convince a roomful of church officials that they needed to build a permanent home for the medical work in a foreign country, it would be George. What he lacked in eloquence or polished people skills, he more than made up for in raw, unbridled enthusiasm.

She heard the engine of the family Model A Ford chug to life. Even the car was a reminder of just how determined her husband could be. When he discovered that the automobile was in storage, waiting for the return of a furloughed missionary, he'd written the owner and offered to buy it even though he didn't have any money. When the gentleman agreed to the sale, George quickly wrote to some of his medical school classmates in the United States and asked them to raise the necessary funds.

Yes, Mickey knew just how persuasive her husband could be. The men at the mission headquarters had might as well start writing checks now.

* * * * *

George looked back at the darkened hospital, its face reflecting the moonlight. A soft glow shone from a few windows as the building's backup generators kept power flowing into the rooms of critically ill patients. It hadn't been as hard a sell as he'd thought it was going to be. The mission officers had fully accepted his dream and looked to him for guidance. Soon, a stately structure began to rise on the crest of the hill crowning the land he'd selected.

* * * * *

The new, two-story, forty-bed Seoul Sanitarium and Hospital opened for business in January 1936. It was six miles from the center of Seoul, just off the main highway, and boasted fireproof, interlocking, concrete-tile construction, a full basement, and a flat roof. It was equipped with X-ray facilities, diathermy, quartz lamps, good sterilization equipment, ample supplies for surgery, and a clinical laboratory.

Seoul Sanitarium and Hospital, Main Building.

The campus included a nurses' dormitory, a foreign-style house for the Rue family, a home for a Korean doctor, and several smaller buildings.

Nurses from Korea who'd recently received training in Shanghai, China, took up their stations throughout the structure while George and his family settled into their comfortable new house. The very first order of business at the facility was to immediately expand its potential.

"I've been waiting and praying about this for a long, long time," said Mildred Watts, whose husband now served as president of the Central Korean Mission, as she gathered supplies in her arms and walked out into the new, polished hallway that led to her simple, but efficient, office. "Your husband is a true godsend."

"I agree," Mickey chuckled.

"No, really," Mildred insisted as the two hurried along the corridor. "I had prayed for a doctor who'd share my vision of starting a school of nursing right here in Korea so we wouldn't have to ship the girls off to China for training." The women rushed through the lobby, waving at other hospital personnel. "Koreans don't consider nursing very professional. We're viewed as servants who have to do all the dirty work. Of course . . . they're right." Mildred laughed softly to herself. "But I found that if I keep my uniform pressed and clean and go about my work with enthusiasm, I'm able to make the profession seem a little less servantlike. I always remind my girls that nursing is a high calling, an important part of the medical work. And, here's the amazing part, your husband agrees. He treats nurses with respect and lets us go about our work with dignity. That's why I'm rushing down this hallway all out of breath with my arms full of operating room supplies. It's all his fault, you know."

Mickey grinned. "Yeah, I know."

"I mean, if it weren't for George, I wouldn't be doing this." The two women paused in front of a door emblazoned with a professionally hand-painted sign that read, *School of Nursing.* "George has his dreams," Mildred said softly. "I have mine."

With that the woman entered the room where ten Korean girls sat quietly waiting to begin their training for a life of medical service. Mickey

Aerial view of Seoul Sanitarium and Hospital. The compound included the main hospital building (upper center) surrounded by an out-patient clinic, OB unit, nurses' dormitory, tuberculosis unit, worker housing, laundry and boiler room, and the church.

stayed in the hallway and quietly closed the door. "Welcome, future nurses," she heard her friend say.

The official opening ceremonies of the hospital were postponed until April to avoid Korea's harsh winter. For Mickey, the festivities carried a special air of excitement because her sweet, gentle George was being recognized for his great achievement. She beamed as she watched him lead tour after tour, showing visiting dignitaries the comfortable rooms, well-equipped labs, and modern operating suite. She could tell by watching him that his heart was overflowing with Christian pride in his accomplishment. This was his moment, and he was savoring it.

But, even as she enjoyed the day, an uncomfortable feeling kept nudging deep inside her abdomen. In the months that followed, the pain became more annoying.

"What did he say?" George asked as she stood just inside his office at the hospital. In the hallway, hurried feet shuffled by as nurses and doctors moved about, busily making people well.

"You were right," Mickey sighed. "Looks like I have an ovarian cyst."

The man rose and walked around his cluttered desk. "Listen to me, Mickey," he said as he wrapped comforting arms about his wife. "There's nothing to worry about. They operate, take out the cyst, and after some follow-up treatment, you're as good as new. We'll schedule the surgery while we're in the States on furlough."

Mickey shook her head. "I was thinking. Didn't you say that Dr. Harry Miller, the physician who runs the training hospital in Shanghai, is coming down this way for a visit?"

"Yes. Miller said he wanted to observe our progress. He travels around as an itinerant surgeon, visiting Adventist hospitals in China, the Philippines, and here in Korea. Dr. Miller spends a few days at each facility, you know, helping with difficult cases, performs thyroidectomies, does some in-service teaching, stuff like that. He also said he wants to explore ways that our two schools of nursing can work more closely together. Mildred is very excited about the possibilities."

Mickey nodded. "So, how about if I ask him to perform my surgery while he's here instead of us waiting until furlough? That way we'll be able to spend more time in the States doing some serious family visiting

Dr. George and Mrs. Mickey Rue, 1936, at the Seoul Sanitarium and Hospital.

and having a nice relaxing time instead of being tied down with my little problem."

George shrugged. "It does make sense, if that's what you want to do. Miller is coming the first of December. You might have to spend a part of Christmas in the hospital."

"Oh, that's not so bad," Mickey stated. "Besides, I'll be able to see our house from my room. You and the children can come visit whenever you want. How 'bout it?"

"I just want you well," the doctor said with a smile. "You've been living with this pain far too long. Your return to good health will be the best Christmas present ever. I can't think of anything I want more."

When Harry Miller, the man known worldwide as "The China Doctor," came to town, Mickey was one of the first patients he examined. Her surgery was performed at the new Seoul Sanitarium and Hospital and went well. A few days later, when Dr. Miller left the country, Mickey was on her way to a full recovery.

But then her fever began to rise. Within hours, a team of concerned medical experts, including her husband, was caring for her around the clock.

"What's happening?" she gasped in agony, barely able to lift her head.

"You have a massive infection from the surgery," George told her, examining her latest chart notations. After a long pause he added, "And . . . and it's spreading out of control. We . . . we can't stop it, Mickey. We just can't."

"George, what does that mean? What's going to happen to me?"

The man's hands trembled as he placed the chart back on its hook at the end of the bed. "It means that . . . it means . . . "

"Am I going to die?" Mickey asked, perspiration washing over her.

George stood for a long moment looking down at the pale, fearful face of his beloved wife. "Yes," he whispered.

Mickey closed her eyes as the horrible news filtered through her pain-dulled thoughts. This wasn't supposed to happen to faithful missionary wives. This wasn't right. It wasn't fair. Men and women who give themselves to service to God are supposed to live long, meaningful lives, filled with hard work and personal sacrifice. They have to do without luxuries and, at times, miss the cultural icons of their home country. They're destined to stand shoulder to shoulder bravely facing every challenge, seeing the mighty hand of their heavenly Father sweep away evil and replace it with good. They're not supposed to die from complications stemming from a routine surgery!

In the midst of her rising anger and fear, Mickey suddenly thought about thirteen-year-old Betty and eleven-year-old George, Jr. She was their mother. They needed her! What would happen to them? How could they face such a horrible loss? Who would help them through this tragedy? Who would say the words they needed to hear; words that would keep them safely in the arms of God during the grief they'd be forced to endure?

And then, she knew. Mickey lifted her hand and touched the arm of her weeping husband. "George," she said. "Bring me a paper and pencil. I have to do something. Hurry, I have to do it now."

That night, with the love of her life standing by her side, Mickey wrote goodbye letters to her two children. Then, in the darkness of her room, comforted by the arms of her sweet husband and sheltered by the presence of the God they both served, Mae Belle Rue died.

The Rue family, 1935.

A few days before Christmas, 1936, George, supported by friends and co-workers, buried the wife of his youth deep in Korean soil in a cemetery near the Han River. As he turned away from the grave, he stumbled and fell, his heart breaking. Loving hands guided him to his knees where he poured out his grief in prayer, pleading with his heavenly Father for strength to carry on. He had a hospital to run and children to raise. And now, he'd have to do it all alone.

At long last, buoyed by the promise that every Christian cherishes—the promise of a new world to come where sickness and death will be forever banished—George stood to his feet, brushed the grass from his knees, and smiled at the loving faces surrounding him. "Come, my friends," he said. "We've got work to do."

Later that day Doctor Rue entered the operating room where a desperately ill patient waited, performed delicate surgery, and then worked most of the night.

Many missionaries return to their home countries after such tragedies. But, Korea had captured George Rue's heart. He remained at his post, immersing himself in his work, giving the impoverished the same level of care he offered to rich merchants and government officials.

An American nurse took up the challenge of mothering Betty and George, Jr., eventually proposing marriage to the dedicated doctor. But George had no interest in giving his heart to anyone but the people of Korea. In time, his heart and the world around him would experience a change. One would be for the good. The other would give birth to unspeakable evil.

A Seat
in the Balcony

George felt a chill run through him, and it wasn't a result of the night air. Memories of those dark days when he'd been forced to stand by helplessly as his sweet wife slipped into the cold arms of death always triggered an emotional shiver deep in his soul.

Young Betty and George, Jr. had also been devastated by the loss. They'd clung to him for support when their hearts were at the breaking point. The three, living so far from family members who would eagerly provide the special comfort only relatives could bring, had to spend their days bravely going about the business of their lives, while at night agonizing tears flowed unseen into the muffled embrace of pillows.

George sighed deeply and gazed up at the stars. He never knew it was possible to experience such emotional pain and yet survive. But he had. And the children had somehow come to grips with the tragedy as well. Together they'd faced the sorrow and moved on, always confident that someday they would all see their precious wife and mother again.

At the front door of his house, George paused. His grief was personal. But the country he'd adopted was, at that same time, experiencing a grief of its own.

* * * * *

"Did you hear what happened?" Ralph Watts, recently appointed president of the Korean Union Mission, called from the doorway.

George looked up from his paperwork and motioned for his friend to enter his small hospital office.

"I was talking with the Korean pastor of a church east of the city," Ralph stated as he lowered himself onto a nearby chair. "He said they had some American missionary visitors over the weekend. Well, the Americans had no more left the property than Japanese authorities descended like the plagues of Egypt. They took the pastor and his head elder down to the police station for some friendly conversation about harboring spies and working to undermine the authority of the entire Japanese Empire. Roughed them up pretty bad. And all he did was entertain a few guests for a couple of hours. Man oh man, I wonder what's going to happen next?"

George nodded. "I really feel sorry for our Korean workers," he said soberly. "As far as the Japanese are concerned, they're employed by the enemy. That's us. They think we're all spies. Now do I look like a spy to you?"

"Yes you do," Ralph responded with a grin. "I think it's the whole doctor thing you've got going here. You know, that stethoscope you wear around your neck all day is really a radio transmitter. And those charts you carry contain top secret military documents. Don't even get me started on that big fountain pen jutting out of your shirt pocket."

"You mean this one?"

"Yeah. Everyone in the spy business knows that's a camera."

George rose and walked toward the door. "Well, this particular spy has rounds to make. The entire Japanese Empire can think whatever they want about me, but if I don't get busy and save a few of their human 'possessions,' they'll have reason to get on my case."

The two friends left the office to attend to the business for which they'd been sent. If the ruling nation considered them spies, that was its problem.

One afternoon in October 1940, as he returned home from a picnic, George received a message from the United States Embassy in Seoul. "American missionaries are being evacuated from Korea, Manchuria, China, and other selected regions," the missive stated. "The Consulate has arranged for the ship *Mariposa* to transport American citizens to the United States. The vessel will be arriving in Inchon after leaving Shanghai."

George folded the note and placed it in his pocket. Betty and George, Jr. were in Shanghai attending school. According to the schedule sent by the consulate, he'd have only a few hours to visit with them before they continued on to America. He had no intention of joining them for the journey.

George and Ralph hurried to the embassy and persuaded the powers that be to let them remain in Korea temporarily while their families made the long voyage home. "The hospital needs us," they explained. But, even as they urged their case, they knew time was running out for all missionaries in that part of the world. They had a feeling, too, that time was also running out for the people of Korea. They were right. World War II was about to explode across their adopted country as it spread its fire around the globe.

Three weeks later, after the *Mariposa* had paused in the harbor to board more foreign passengers and then continue eastward, Ralph found George sitting in the darkened attic of the Rue house hunched over the short-wave radio. "Anything yet?" Ralph asked as he squatted down beside him.

"Nothing."

The man fingered the knobs and dials as raspy static and random squeals and crackles filled the room. "They should have arrived by now. But the oceans aren't exactly safe. Any number of problems could have delayed the *Mariposa*."

Ralph chuckled softly. "Man, you've got guts. Short-wave radios are *illegal* in this country. Only the Japanese have them. Now, here we are in your attic with an antenna strung around the rafters and a contraband radio on the floor!"

Suddenly a voice crackled from the tiny speaker, ". . . have a special guest this evening who'd like to speak to friends in a certain foreign country."

Another man's voice filled the room. After a moment of listening, George gasped. "Hey, isn't that the guy we met at Inchon, you know, when the *Mariposa* came through? Yeah. That's him. I recognize the accent. He said he'd try to get a message to us when he reached California."

Ralph leaned forward. "I believe you're right. That means the ship made it all the way to San Francisco safely! This is good news! Our families are OK. They're OK!"

". . . And I have a special message from GHR's children," the voice in the radio called out across the miles. "Tell GHR that his children arrived safely and that their aunt and uncle met them at the docks."

A big smile creased George's face. "Hallelujah!" he cried. "Betty and George, Jr. are back in the States, probably eating ice cream even as we speak."

Ralph beamed over at his friend as both men's hearts rejoiced at the wonderful news that their loved ones were finally out of harm's way.

The next day, George had a surprise visitor. An official from the Japanese Consulate in Seoul, dressed in a dark suit and shiny shoes, stood before him. Stepping forward smartly and then bowing, the man announced, "We are fully aware that all missionaries are leaving Korea. But we respectfully request that you, Doctor Rue, remain. We know you are not politically minded. The people need you. *We* need you. Please stay."

George was taken back by the request. "I would like to accommodate you," he responded as he returned the bow, showing the visitor that his presence was accepted. "But I must get in touch with the head of my organization and do whatever they advise."

"I understand," the consul responded, returning the bow. "But please consider my request." With that he turned on his heels and was gone.

Church officials in Singapore gave George and Ralph permission to remain "for a time" as the political climate continued to evolve. But by the spring of 1941, the men in charge of Church operations in Asia felt conditions were moving from bad to worse and advised the two missionaries to leave Korea as soon as possible.

The only passage the two could book on such short notice was on a Japanese freighter. This choice caused eyebrows to rise at the American Embassy, but under the circumstances, leaving was the better part of valor.

During the long voyage to the United States, George glanced out the porthole of his stateroom every morning and checked the sun's position to make sure that the ship was still heading east, toward America.

Doctor Rue had left the hospital in good hands. The Korean staff continued to operate the facility under the able leadership of S. Y. Chung, MD.

As the winds of war grew into a gale-force hurricane, national workers and church members were forced to flee the city. Many found refuge in the mountains. German missionaries who'd chosen to remain in the area were rounded up and sent to concentration camps in Japan.

The Empire of the Rising Sun took over the hospital in 1943, turning it into a tuberculosis facility.

While World War II raged around the globe, Doctor Rue joined forces with Dr. John A. Wahlen, a 1924 graduate and fellow classmate of the College of Medical Evangelists. He worked at Wahlen's medical practice in Montebello, California, a suburb of Los Angeles. George's patients loved him. His cheerful and friendly spirit made him many new friends.

As the war years slipped by, Betty and George, Jr. became full-fledged adults. Betty fell in love with and married a man named Leland Mitchell. They eagerly set up a home of their own.

Shortly after George had arrived back in the United States, a letter from the General Conference Committee notified him that one of its regular meetings had taken an action that provided "permanent return" status for missionaries on furlough or as evacuees from the orient. His name was on the list.

But the letter left the door of opportunity wide open. "While you are not, I think, expecting to return to the Far East in the immediate future," the message advised, "I am writing this word to let you know that in using this expression 'permanent return' in connection with the status of our missionaries who are unable, in view of world conditions, to return for the present to their respective fields, we have it in mind that when the way clears for them to do so they will be at the call of their respective divisions."

In a letter to W. P. Bradley of the General Conference, dated October 7, 1945, Doctor Rue wrote, "I am glad to be able to say that if and when the way opens up, I'm willing and eager to return to Korea." In a follow-up letter sent a week and a half later, George added, "I hope that a real strong work can be built up, much stronger than it was before."

As the horrific winds of war subsided and the Japanese Empire crumbled into ruins, Doctor Rue received the word he'd been waiting for. The General Conference Committee had decided that, at long last, he could return to his beloved Korea.

George started making plans immediately. He had much to do in order to wrap up his work in Montebello. He spent the winter months gathering equipment and supplies and preparing his heart and body for the work he knew lay ahead. He'd heard that his beloved Seoul lay in ruins. He could only imagine what would greet him on his return to the hospital.

But fate had a couple more cards to play as George set his sights back on his adopted country.

Early one Sabbath morning, in the spring of 1946, a nurse by the name of Grace Lea entered the White Memorial Seventh-day Adventist Church in Los Angeles. The sanctuary was crowded with regular members as well as medical personnel and staff from nearby White Memorial Hospital. Grace had some difficulty finding a place to sit, but finally settled in the balcony next to some friends and prepared to enjoy the church service.

If she'd glanced over her shoulder, she would have noticed two men sitting nearby, Bibles open across their laps, listening to the soft music echoing from the organ. One was Dr. Wahlen, who sat with his wife nestled close to him. Beside them was a distinguished-looking man with short, slightly wavy gray hair and carefully clipped mustache. He was trim and smartly dressed; tie expertly tied under a starched and very white collar.

She never noticed the second physician. But he certainly noticed her. He appreciated the fact that she carried herself with dignity and poise. Her soft, blond hair was piled neatly on her head with curled strands resting comfortably against the back of her neck.

The very next day, her phone rang.

"Grace Lea," she answered.

"Hi, Grace. This is Eileen Wahlen."

"Oh, hi."

"Listen, Doctor George Rue, my husband's partner, saw you at church yesterday and asked me to see if he might contact you . . . you know, take you out for dinner?"

"You mean George Rue as in *Korea* George Rue?"

"Yes, that's him. He inquired about you and would like your phone number and address. He's kind of formal, a widower as you may know. I think you two would enjoy each other's company. So, would it be OK if I passed on your information to him?"

Grace replied, "Sure. I'll be happy to talk to him. Have him call me. My schedule is kind of busy so, if I don't answer, tell him to keep trying."

Mrs. Wahlen let out a sigh of relief. "Oh, thank you, Grace. We all took particular notice when George asked me to call you. He's professional to the core, but once you get to know him, he's a very kind and gentle man. Somewhat soft spoken, so you may have to carry a conversation or two."

"Just tell him to get in touch with me. We'll find things to talk about. I know, I'll ask him about Korea. That should do the trick."

After Grace gave her address to the woman on the other end of the line, she heard her say, "He's really a good man, Grace. I think you'll enjoy his company."

Grace smiled as she hung up the phone. George Rue. Of course she'd heard of him. Everyone at White Memorial had. He enjoyed the deep respect of many of his fellow Adventists for his selfless, missionary-minded work in far away Korea.

A couple of days later, a carefully handwritten letter arrived. It was from George. He invited Grace to join him for dinner.

Their first meeting was cordial and most pleasant. George was everything Mrs. Wahlen had said he'd be—attentive, interesting, and very professional. Grace was impressed by his seemingly endless knowledge on a number of different subjects. But his favorite topic centered on a small country located in the Far East—Korea.

George and Grace developed a closer friendship over the next few months. Grace even accepted a position in the same office, but working for a different physician. Their conduct in and around the workplace was strictly professional.

One day, just as Grace was arriving at work, Dr. Wahlen addressed his staff. Everyone could tell that the man had something serious to share.

"I'm afraid I have some bad news," he said somberly. "It's George. He . . . he's been in an accident in Arizona." An audible gasp filled the office. "As you know, he was on his way to the General Conference session in Washington, D.C. Well, the driver of a cross-country semi-truck fell asleep at the wheel. He woke up just as he was about to plow into a bridge abutment. To avoid hitting the bridge, he swerved hard to one side, right into Doctor Rue's car. George was pinned inside the wreckage with the left side of his skull crushed. I'm afraid it cut a nerve. He's being transferred by train back here to Montebello with his arm in a sling and experiencing a lot of pain. Poor George. He isn't going to have feeling on the left side of his face for the rest of his life. And, there'll be a slight paralysis."

The day after Doctor Rue arrived in Montebello, Wahlen's office nurse approached Grace. "I'm going to the hospital to visit George. Would you like to come along?"

Grace nodded. "Yes," she said. "I feel I should go see him as well, and I'd be glad to have you with me."

When the two women entered the hospital room, they found their friend lying in bed experiencing a lot of discomfort. One whole side of his face was black and blue, and an ugly, stitched cut ran across his scalp. His left arm hung in a sling and was very swollen.

Without even thinking, Grace reached out and started to massage his injured arm carefully, lightly. At first George winced, then a painful smile lifted the corners of his lips. "Hey, that feels pretty good," he said. "Yes, I believe that's helping to relieve some of the ache. Thank you."

But Grace's kindness and gentle touch was affecting more than his hurting arm. It was reaching into his lonely heart, stimulating a growing interest in the woman he'd first seen at church.

During subsequent times together in the following months,
George talked endlessly about
Korea, asking Grace if she might
enjoy the various activities found
there, even suggesting that she
should pay the country a visit. He
remained vague, never asking direct questions. Grace fully understood her friend's love for the
people of Korea. She knew the
dedication that drove him, a de-
votion that filled his every waking
hour. "I've given my heart to that
country," he'd often say. "I promised the Lord that I will always belong there."

Dr. George and Mrs. Grace Rue, 1946.

One evening, George stopped being vague. Turning to Grace he said
without fanfare or emotion, "Will you marry me and go with me to
Korea?"

Grace spoke the words she'd prepared for just such a question. "Yes,
George, I'll marry you," she said. "And I'll go wherever God wants me
to go."

Shortly thereafter, the two attended Betty's graduation from the
St. Helena Sanitarium and Hospital School of Nursing in the beautiful
Napa Valley north of San Francisco and then departed for Colorado.
After waiting three days for a marriage license, George Henry Rue, age
47, married soft-spoken Zilda Grace Lea, age 36, at a simple ceremony
at Grace's parents' home in Grand Junction. It was October 31, 1945, a
month after the Japanese had signed surrender papers aboard the Battleship Missouri in Tokyo Harbor.

The couple drove to Portland, Oregon, to visit George's mother for
a few days, then headed back to Southern California to complete prepa-
rations for their journey to Korea.

On Thanksgiving Day, the Rues checked into a hotel in San Francisco and tried to book passage on the first ship headed for Korea. While

they waited, they spent much time watching for sales on supplies that they knew the hospital would need on their return. George and Grace set their minds and hearts to the task before them. War-torn Korea waited beyond the western horizon.

But the country George had left years before was going to be a very different place when he returned. Just how different would become agonizingly clear the moment his ship sailed into Inchon harbor.

* * * * *

George glanced again in the direction of the darkened hospital. The war years had taken a terrible toll, not only on the country of Korea but on its peace-loving people. After the shooting had stopped and the bombs no longer dropped from the sky, the citizens of this proud country had stumbled to their feet and shaken the dust from their clothes. Resolutely, they'd wiped years of tears from their eyes and set their minds to the task of rebuilding their devastated towns, cities, and lives.

But, even as they labored to rebuild, there were forces at work that would soon sweep over the battered country once again.

* * * * *

After Japan's defeat in World War II, Korea looked for a quick liberation under the Cairo Declaration of 1943. It gave hope to the Korean people that eventually they would experience freedom and self-determination. The United States, China, and Russia pledged to support their long-sought-after independence.

However, a meeting of the Allies in Yalta in February 1945, led to an agreement that would eventually split Korea in half. Russia and the United States divided Korea at the thirty-eighth parallel. North Korea held approximately 58 percent of the land and one third of the population. North Korea and most of the country's industries came under Russian influence and protection. It was renamed the Democratic People's Republic of Korea.

Largely agricultural South Korea came under American influence and protection and became known as the Republic of Korea. Seoul, the new capital, boasted nearly 75 percent of the population. The economy also was split leaving South Korea dependant on the North for its electricity needs.

The horror of World War II spared nothing. Families had been ripped apart as parents were murdered, leaving thousands of orphans roaming the streets. Enemy marauders pillaged the country's resources. The Seoul Sanitarium and Hospital had been gutted and valuable equipment and instruments stolen. Inflation soared. Millions of homeless lived in tents, makeshift homes, and caves.

Unfortunately for the missionaries eager to return to their adopted country, only a few women who had previously resided in Korea were allowed visas. This meant that George must leave his new bride behind. While Doctor Rue and his friend and coworker Ralph Watts waited for their ship to sail, they visited all the stores and shops in San Francisco to purchase hospital supplies, including linens.

During this time, Betty's young husband, Leland Mitchell, overheard a conversation between George and Ralph about the need to rebuild mission facilities. Leland took everyone by surprise by announcing, "Hey, I'll go. I'll be glad to help get the work started again." The General Conference quickly and thankfully accepted his offer.

It took George a full five months to secure the necessary permits and travel arrangements. In the meantime, Ralph and Mildred Watts caught a plane to Korea, leaving both their freight and automobile for Doctor Rue to bring later. As he took up his new duties, Ralph wrote back, outlining in detail the hard times the nation was facing. His last communication urged George to hurry. "Be sure to bring the automobiles," he stated. "Travel is almost impossible unless you walk or have your own transportation."

Finally, on April 15, 1947, Doctor Rue headed west across the wide Pacific Ocean, along with his son-in law, Leland Mitchell, who was to be the industrial arts teacher at the college and oversee the rebuilding of damaged houses and facilities at the Korean Union Mission; James Lee, who was to start the higher education work in the country; several Korean men who'd been attending the General Conference session; and R. S. Lee, the Union educational secretary.

Other missionaries making plans to travel to Korea around this time included Robert C. Mills, newly appointed treasurer of the Korean Union Mission, and George Munson, assigned to be manager of the publishing house.

Most of the wives of all these men were not permitted into the country except a few who had been there before, such as Mrs. Watts. Betty stayed with Leland Mitchell's parents in Pomona, California, while Grace attended Korean language school in Berkeley until it came time for her to leave for Korea.

George and his fellow travelers came ashore at Inchon with truckloads of medical supplies jammed in a landing craft. An Army jeep carried him the thirty or so miles to his beloved hospital compound north of Seoul.

The war had left the city virtually flattened except for a few large buildings. Those that still stood had had their windows completely blown out. Bombs and gunfire had severed tree limbs. Roads were bordered with barbed wire, forcing travelers to drive in the middle of the street. There was another reason not to stray too far afield. Live land mines lined both sides of most of the avenues and roads.

Reaching the perimeter of the hospital campus, George hopped out of the jeep and then walked to the gate house. Slowly he climbed the fifty yards of rising grounds until he stood staring up at the two-story remains of what was once his pride and joy—the hospital itself. He nudged a piece of rubble off the walk with his toe and stood there with his hands in his pockets, evaluating the grim scene.

Most men would feel overwhelming discouragement at a time like this. But not George Rue. He wasn't even close to discouragement. His thoughts were focused on starting over. It would take hard work. And he knew he'd need a lot of help.

As he entered the hospital, former employees ran to greet him, opening their arms wide to the man who'd established the medical work in their beloved city. They were on the job, walking through the rubble of war each day, trying to keep from stepping on deadly land mines, laboring to get the hospital ready to begin caring for patients again.

When one of the national workers, Rena Chung, heard of Doctor Rue's return, she hid in the operating room so he would not see her tears of joy. Looking about at the smiling faces, George asked, "Where's Rena?"

"She was here just a moment ago," someone responded.

George smiled. "Then I must find her."

Rena, who loved Doctor Rue and the fatherly kindness he'd brought into her life, cried loud and long when she saw him. His presence could mean only one thing—the years of war, of bloodshed, of untold horrors had truly come to an end. Their reunion brought tears of joy to all that witnessed it.

The Japanese had stripped the institution bare, leaving the laboratories empty and valuable equipment and instruments nowhere to be found. Four towels and a pair of surgeon's gloves were all that remained in what had been one of the most modern and well-equipped hospitals in Seoul.

George grinned broadly as his Korean counterparts showed him the empty shelves and storage rooms. "Don't worry," he said. "I'm home again, and I've brought with me our church's response to this terrible tragedy."

The graduates from the Seoul Sanitarium and Hospital nursing program, November 1949. Miss Irene Robson, director of nurses, is in the center on the first row.

A week later, as soon as some of his supplies arrived at the hospital, George opened the medical unit. Within a few short months, the Seoul Sanitarium and Hospital was fully operational, boasting an occupancy rate of more than 100 percent.

As medical director of the Seoul Sanitarium and Hospital, George and his team had reestablished the Seventh-day Adventist medical work in Korea. In November of that same year, the School of Nursing opened its doors wide once again.

Three months after Doctor Rue's arrival, Grace, along with Betty, who was eight months pregnant, climbed aboard the very first scheduled Northwest Airlines flight to Korea after World War II. Only six or eight passengers joined them as they eagerly winged their way across the Pacific from Alaska.

When the aircraft arrived over the fog-hidden Aleutian Islands, the pilot was informed that, because of low clouds, they were being denied permission to land and refuel. So, the airman followed the only option open to him. He turned the plane around and flew all the way back to Anchorage with barely thirty minutes of fuel remaining.

Three days later the pilot received clearance to fly as far as Japan. All during this time, Grace and Betty had no way of communicating with their husbands in Seoul.

The flight arrived in Japan early in the evening but too late to continue on until the next day. The women were taken to a U.S. Army base to spend the night.

In the morning the pilot flew them to another air base in Japan, where he attempted to get permission to make the short hop to Korea. He told his passengers that he would be gone for only a few minutes and asked them to wait in the plane. As time passed and the summer sun heated the inside of the aircraft to unbearable temperatures, the sweating passengers abandoned ship and hurried inside the Army store to wait for further word. At 4:55 P.M., the pilot reappeared and breathlessly called to his passengers, "Come quick, come!" He ran to the plane with his charges stumbling after him not knowing what the big rush was about.

It wasn't until the aircraft was approaching Seoul that the pilot announced that he was landing *without permission* and that he had had to take off from Japan before 5 P.M. in order to make the journey. He was bound and determined to get Betty to Korea before her baby was born because, if the child had been born in Japan, both mother and infant would have been unable to get a permit to enter Korea.

Finally, with a screech of tires, the Northwest Airlines flight arrived at a military airport near Seoul . . . four days late.

During those four days Doctor Rue, Leland Mitchell, and some of the other missionaries had taken turns staying at the airport, anxiously awaiting the women's arrival. On this day, because no planes were expected to land after 5 P.M., most had decided to leave. But Mitchell felt impressed to stay by. The minute the long-overdue plane touched down at 6:45 P.M., the skies opened up and dumped a very wet rain squall on everyone. Two weeks later, Leland and Betty became the proud parents of Doctor Rue's first granddaughter, Barbara.

Life looked promising again. The hospital work was flourishing, the Korean Union Mission was fully staffed and operational, missionary houses were being rebuilt, the education work was shifting into high gear, and the winds of war had finally subsided.

When Grace first arrived, George insisted that she not work. "You can be a housewife," he promised. But three days later, he was in need of someone to go into Seoul on hospital business.

"I haven't been through town in the daytime," Grace told him when he came to her with his request. "But, if you'll draw me a map of the city, naming the streets, I'll give it a try."

After that, Grace headed into town almost every day on hospital business. After several months, George kept his promise and arranged for an employee to make the daily journeys into town.

* * * * *

Now, much later, as Doctor George Rue looked out over the darkened compound of the Seoul Sanitarium and Hospital with its School of Nursing and rooms filled with trusting patients, he felt uneasy. Life had a way of fooling you. Just as everything seemed to be going smoothly, something new and disturbing would bring everything crashing down.

George shook his head as if to clear his mind of such thoughts. The God he served didn't dwell on the negative. The Bible was filled with promises and endless words of encouragement. The Communists holding North Korea in an icy grip might be able to turn the power on and off, but they couldn't diminish his love for God and the people he'd traveled halfway around the world to serve. If circumstances forced him to operate by *candlelight,* he'd do it! God's work must go forward. As long as he was drawing breath and people were looking to him for leadership, he'd never give up.

With one last glance toward the dark horizon, he turned and entered his house. "Grace? Grace?" He called into the shadows. "I'm home."

The Four-Cornered Wall

George stood in the kitchen doorway savoring the smell of fresh buttered toast and hot chocolate. The first rays of dawn were just beginning to drift over the rice paddies surrounding the hospital campus as a new day moved in from the east.

"Our hospital generator sure has been getting a workout these past few months," he said as he seated himself at the breakfast table. "I've tried to schedule surgeries in the early mornings, not only because it's cooler then but because I can also expect some light through the windows and in the hallways. The trouble is, I can't always be sure that some emergency won't pop up and I'll have to do some cutting after the sun goes down. Sickness and disease aren't even attempting to work in cooperation with the whims of the Communists to our north."

Grace grinned. "Not a big chance of that happening anytime soon," she said, seating herself across from her husband. "But, you're certainly doing your part to fight back. You're on the job at six o'clock every morning, work sixteen-hour days seeing up to seventy-five patients, teach medical classes, make life miserable for the interns with your endless questioning of their every diagnosis, and then perform rounds in the evening after dinner."

George dropped a piece of buttered toast onto his plate and reached for another slice. "Tuberculosis, malnutrition, intestinal parasites; there's a lot of sickness in Korea right now, my dear. How can I turn my back on all that's going on?"

Grace sighed. "Can I at least get you to eat your meals on a regular basis?"

George shook his head. "You know I can't walk out the door in front of people who've been waiting all day to see me," he countered.

"Ah-ha! I knew that's what you'd say," Grace triumphed. "That's why I've made some arrangements."

"Arrangements?"

"Yes. I've asked your office nurse, Rena, to reserve an examining room everyday at lunch time. You can pick up an armload of charts and head that direction looking, for all the world, like a dedicated physician about to see a patient. But, instead of someone waiting for you with a terrible disease or ailment, you'll find me standing there with a healthful lunch spread out on the examining table, and you'll sit down and eat a regular meal like regular people."

"How can I fight such skillful manipulation?" George said with a gentle smile. "Now, while we're on the subject, let's talk about *your* activities. Let's see, you're the hospital supply officer, liaison with the United States Army and American Embassy, and keep two secretaries busy full time. Oh, and you've now taken on the responsibility of being the meal police on my behalf. Anything I missed?"

Grace smiled over at her husband. "Yes. I'm also your loving wife, very best friend, trustworthy confidante, *and* meal police."

George ate in silence for a few minutes. When he spoke again, it was between bites. "They won't let me have my morgue."

"Who won't?"

"The men at the Korean Union Mission. They insist I'm spending far too much money at the hospital. Said I've run up such a debt that the Far Eastern Division is on their case."

"Operating a medical facility is expensive," Grace stated. "I'm sure they understand that."

"I *need* that morgue. I want to build it down by the gate so that ambulances won't have to drive up to the hospital. It'll make the whole operation much more efficient."

Grace rose to her feet. "Well, maybe next year," she said as she headed for the sink. "After all, the Union has budgets to keep and only so much money. I'm sure George Munson has his hands out for the publishing work, the two Lee's are trying to fund an education program, and who knows what other expenses the organization has to cover. The hospital is just one of many ongoing projects in need of financial help."

"They said I could build a wall."

"A wall?"

"Yeah. I mentioned that I wanted to have an eight-foot-high security perimeter wall built below the hospital, you know, down by the road. I asked for a morgue and all the Union will give me is a silly . . ." George stopped talking mid-bite.

Grace glanced over at her husband. "You were saying?"

The doctor laid down his spoon and got up slowly. "What are you thinking?" Grace asked.

A smile spread across George's face. Turning to his wife he said cheerily. "Oh, nothing. See you. I've got to go build a wall."

The contractor he'd hired for the project arrived later that day. George was at the gatehouse to greet him.

"Here's what you're going to do," he announced to the builder. "You'll start your cement wall down there as indicated on the drawings. When you get to this spot here by the gatehouse, turn the wall ninety degrees to the right." The contractor made some notations on a pad of paper as George paced across the dry earth. "Proceed twelve feet to here. Then turn ninety degrees to the right again, proceed twelve more feet, and then turn ninety degrees to the right one more time. Connect this wall to that wall over there."

The contractor scratched his head. "You want me to build this way, then this way, then this way, then this way?"

"Exactly. When you're finished, put an opening right here facing the road."

"What's going on?" the man asked, trying to imagine the four-sided structure rising up from the ground. "You building a new gatehouse?"

George shook his head. "No. After I get some excess roofing material and a door, I'll have built myself a morgue!"

Within a few weeks, ambulance drivers summoned to transport the bodies of patients who'd passed away during their stay at the hospital didn't have to disrupt the traffic circling in front of the facility any more. They simply stopped opposite the gatehouse at a new morgue that looked very much like part of a security wall. Without attracting so much as a glance from people passing by, they left with their silent cargo safely tucked away in the back of their vehicles.

The need for heightened security wasn't a luxury in post-war Korea. It was a necessity. One morning Ralph Watts told a gathering of missionaries that, the night before, someone had come into his mission compound house while he and Mildred were sleeping. The thief had climbed onto the porch roof and entered the couple's bedroom where he stole Ralph's clothes that were lying neatly on a chair by his bed, left his own dirty clothes in their place, and slipped away totally undetected.

Just a few nights later, while George and Grace were taking inventory in the hospital, uninvited guests entered the Rue residence as well. They removed an entire storm window and a pane of glass from the living room window and proceeded to steal the chiming clock from the mantle above the fireplace and helped themselves to some clothes and Grace's purse containing about fifty dollars. Betty; her husband, Leland; baby Barbara; and the Rue German Shepherd dog were upstairs at the time sound asleep.

In spite of the ever-present financial challenges facing Doctor Rue and his hospital, he managed to expand the medical ministry. When he returned to Korea in 1947, the grounds contained eight buildings. In 1949 it boasted twenty-four structures that housed nine families and fifteen single women. He added another floor to the nurses' dormitory, bringing total occupancy to sixty, and oversaw the construction of a thirty-five-resident dormitory for men, a laundry, a boiler room, and a medical unit for thirty patients.

In keeping with the spiritual theme driving the hospital's outreach, he'd also built a church by the road below the medical center, calling it "The Rue Memorial Chapel" in loving honor of his first wife, Mickey. Doctor Rue's office nurse and good friend, Rena Chung, was the first to be married in the new sanctuary. Out of appreciation for her years of dedicated service, George and Grace paid all her wedding expenses.

Doctor Rue also installed a central heating system in the hospital, making the facility much more comfortable while adding greatly to his responsibilities. "I'm the maintenance man," he wrote to friends back in the United States. "If any problems arise with the physical plant, I have to fix them."

The growing facility with its sterling reputation, well-trained staff, and team of nurses all dressed in starched, white cotton uniforms that made them appear like angels hovering beside the beds, caught the eye of the United States State Department as well. In order to meet the medical needs of Americans in Korea, the department requested that various mission hospitals reserve a certain number of beds for State use. In exchange, they'd help rebuild and equip the facilities. The Seoul Sanitarium and Hospital cheerfully reserved fifteen beds under that arrangement and enjoyed the added financial boost.

Doctor Rue's work became well known throughout Korea. Patients even traveled from the Russian-dominated area north of the thirty-eighth parallel at great personal risk in order to make use of the facility. Closer to home, the man in charge of the Standard Oil Company in Seoul who'd been acquainted with the Church's work in China, asked George for some "Adventist pork chops," a type of food he liked very much. The doctor obliged, happily providing cans of the soy-based meat substitute.

Recognizing growing medical needs and opportunities in Korea, George was instrumental in getting Americans Meade Baldwin, a dentist, and Ralph Pearson, M.D., to join the staff. He told friends that he truly enjoyed having fellow countrymen with which to counsel and discuss difficult cases.

One day as Rena Chung sat resting on a blanket in the shade of a tree below the hospital, enjoying the summer breezes blowing across the well-kept campus, a group of nursing students approached. "Rena," one said as they flopped down beside her on the cool grass, "tell us

*Dr. Rue (first row, center) with a group of doctors, nurses, and
student nurses at the Seoul Sanitarium and Hospital.*

about Doctor Rue. We see him working with patients, and he's taught a
few of our classes, but we really don't know that much about him. You've
known him for a long time. What's he like?"

Rena thought for a moment, savoring the many memories she'd collected from past interaction with her beloved friend. "Well," she began,
"as you know, he's a fine physician. Very skilled."

"Yes, we've seen him in action," the students agreed. "But, what's he
like as a person?"

Rena nodded. "Recently I went with Doctor Rue to see a man living
in a cave."

"A cave?" the group gasped.

"Yes. The Japanese had taken everything from him, leaving him with
no home or family. He lives in a cave, barely able to keep himself alive.
Well, he got sick, and word reached the hospital that he needed help.
Doctor Rue grabbed his medical bag, gathered some extra medicines,
and asked me to go along as he went to help treat the poor gentleman.
We found him right where everyone said he'd be, lying on the dirt floor
of a cave, terribly ill. Doctor Rue went to work, examining him, asking
him questions through me, treating the man as if he were the most

important patient in the world. I remember standing there, watching a doctor who cares for rich and famous people and is usually surrounded by the most modern medical equipment available, kneel on a dirt floor and work by the dim light of a lantern as he treated the poorest of the poor. He had no thought of his own comfort. And there was no way this guy would be able to pay for the care he was getting. But Doctor Rue went right on, treating the man with respect as if he were a king. I remember thinking to myself, *The Lord has sent Doctor Rue to Korea.*"

"And how about the guy with the lice?" the students urged, edging closer.

"Oh, yes," the nurse responded with a shudder. "One day a beggar with tattered and filthy clothes came in for treatment. His body odor made us sick to our stomachs. Nobody wanted to touch him. When Doctor Rue helped him take off his shirt, we noticed that the man was completely covered with lice. It was terrible! But the doctor didn't seem to notice. He ran his hand over the patient's body, on his back and chest, as if nothing were wrong. Doctor Rue didn't change his method of examination one bit, even though the patient was in such an awful and repulsive condition. I don't think I could have done what he did. We were all truly amazed.

"But, that's just his way. He puts his patients first and treats each with a sense of personal dignity and respect, making them feel comfortable and accepted."

Rena paused. "This is very evident when shy Korean women come in for examination. As you know, our traditional dress can include up to ten layers of cloth. When the women have removed three or four of them, Doctor Rue will make a funny comment or tell a funny story to make them laugh. They quickly forget their embarrassment. It's fascinating to watch him put these ladies at ease with his kind smile and professional attention to their needs."

"How does he do it?" one of the students asked. "What makes it possible for him to treat everyone so equally?"

"Doctor Rue is always talking about the Great Physician . . . you know, God. He says he wants to be like Him. Well, I think he does a pretty good job. He makes us all feel very special. Sometimes Doctor Rue and his wife will take groups of us nurses to visit the beach or we'll pile in the Rue car and head for town to attend an opera. We have a great time. It's as if we're all part of the same family—like brothers and sisters."

Rena rose to her feet and brushed grass clippings from her crisp, starched uniform. "Hey, I've got to go. You see, Doctor Rue also insists that his nurses be punctual and take *their* jobs seriously, just like he does." As she turned to leave, she stopped and looked back at the group of young nursing students. "He's human," she said. "He makes mistakes. I've seen him get frustrated and angry. But if I were ever sick or in need of medical attention, I'd come to Doctor Rue first. As far as I'm concerned, he's the best physician in Korea. The very best."

With that, she made her way up the steps leading to the hospital waiting at the crest of the hill.

The Seventh-day Adventist Church in Korea grew rapidly as the 1950s began. The hospital business manager suggested to Doctor Rue that the facility would need more room to expand in the future and that property should be purchased before prices increased. He investigated the possibility of buying a piece of land adjacent to the hospital, only to learn that fifteen different people owned it! This, of course, complicated the transaction, but the hospital eventually purchased it after some heavy praying and lots of diplomacy.

Dozens of squatters inhabited another parcel that the facility needed. Knowing the difficulty and sensitive nature of uprooting such desperate people, George decided to seek help from a friend and regular patient who also happened to be the president of South Korea, Syngman Rhee. Grace was given the task of personally delivering a petition on the subject to the high official's office. In the lobby, she ran into the president's wife. "Well, what brings you here?" Mrs. Rhee asked with an inviting smile.

"We're hoping the president can assist us in obtaining a piece of property," Grace explained, showing the woman the petition.

"Come," the First Lady urged. "I'll show you where he is myself."

Grace presented the petition and explained her request. President Rhee knew of the property because several other organizations were trying their best to purchase it too. The Korean leader promised his visitor that he'd give the matter some thought and have his wife call her later when he'd developed a plan of action. Eventually, the Seoul Sanitarium and Hospital purchased the twenty-seven acres for $27,000. With President Rhee's blessing, they gave four acres to the squatters.

Through all the turmoil and challenges of practicing medicine in unusual circumstances, Doctor Rue's sense of humor continued to emerge. He often acknowledged his inability to write a simple letter without an abundance of typing errors.

In one such missive he wrote, "If it should happen that there were no mistakes in this letter, you would not recognize it as coming from me." The word *coming* had a *j* superimposed over the *n* followed by two *g*'s.

"This is the second time I've typed this," he admitted as the letter continued. "My first stencils [the forerunner of carbon paper] were all right, but the printing was so bad that none of you would be able to make it out. Since they threw the stencils away after making the mimeographs [copies from the stencils], I had to write the whole thing over again. I started this letter February 5, and here it is March 13."

Life in and around the hospital was a whirlwind of activity, keeping everyone on his or her toes. But, even as George and Grace labored with the medical work, and their longtime friend Ralph Watts spearheaded the evangelistic, ministerial, educational, and publishing outreach of the Seventh-day Adventist Church in South Korea, powerful forces to the north were gathering like clouds over a mountain. As the summer sun of 1950 warmed the tanned faces and the rice paddies of a nation, a tempest was about to burst across the peaceful countryside, and no one would escape the cataclysm.

Precious Cargo

"I'll see you soon." George hugged his wife as the two stood beside the large airliner being readied for flight on the ramp of Seoul's Kimpo Airport. Behind them, passengers climbed aboard, eager to begin their journey toward San Francisco. "You keep yourself busy with your duties at the hospital while I attend the General Conference Session in California. I'll be back before you know it. There's no need to worry, OK?"

With a final goodbye kiss, George quickly bounded up the steps of the transport. Grace saw him turn, wave, and mouth the words, "You'll be fine." Then he moved inside.

On Sunday, June 25, around 4:30 P.M., President Rhee's wife was sitting in a dental chair in the hospital being fitted for a new set of dentures when she was called to the phone. Grace happened by just as the First Lady hung up. Mrs. Rue noticed a frightened look in her friend's eyes.

"I . . . I have to go," Mrs. Rhee said as she hurried down the hallway. "I must return home immediately." With that, she disappeared out the door.

Other phones began to ring throughout Seoul as the American Embassy started spreading the word to all American non-military personnel known to be living in the city. "Women and children are being

70

evacuated," staffers announced. "Be ready to come to the Embassy within an hour of our call. Each person will be permitted one suitcase and one blanket. Nothing more."

Unseen by the frightened missionaries and other American citizens throughout South Korea was the sight of thousands of Communist soldiers pouring over the thirty-eighth parallel—their faces, guns, and tanks pointed south.

When the order to evacuate came to the Korean Union Mission compound, several wives almost went into hysteria. Their husbands were two hundred miles away, up near the North Korean border, dedicating a new Seventh-day Adventist church in the town of Kangnung. They'd left two days before, on Friday, June 23.

The men's 1949 Ford had had a rough time navigating the mountain roads built primarily for bull carts and high-axle Japanese-made trucks. Americans E.W. Bahr, James Lee, George Munson, and Robert Mills, along with Korean worker Oh Young Sup, had enjoyed the Sabbath hours with the new congregation and were now getting ready to attend a Sunday morning meeting when news reached them that Kangnung was under martial law. At two o'clock that afternoon, they began hearing gunfire to the north. "There have been three landings of North Korean forces along the Kangnung coast," an American military adviser stationed in the area told them. "You'd better leave immediately. This isn't a simple border skirmish. An army is on the move, and they are heading straight toward Seoul."

With artillery shells exploding along the nearby coast, and the steady beat of a pouring rain hampering their every move, the men hurriedly loaded their car. Soon they were skidding down muddy mountain roads, doing their best to dodge advancing and retreating military vehicles. High amounts of adrenaline and the mighty hand of God would be needed to get them to Seoul before the Communists.

They skidded into the mission compound at 2:30 A.M. and were greeted by terrified wives. Fifteen minutes later, the American missionaries were on their way to the center of Seoul, ready to join the waiting convoy of vehicles at the Embassy motor pool. They left behind everything they owned except what would squeeze into their suitcases.

Grace had spent Sunday evening in surgery where five gravely wounded patients had been brought in from the fighting. Every doctor and nurse was on high alert, working feverishly late into the night. At midnight, final word came in. "Go to the American Embassy as quickly as possible."

Grace made arrangements with business manager Kim Eung to contact the foreign families living at the nearby college and have them brought to the hospital.

Before leaving the medical compound, Grace made her way in the darkness to the women's dormitory and, with tears in her eyes, kissed each sleeping nurse goodbye. She didn't know whether she would ever see them again.

Her heart was breaking. These precious people had survived the horrors of World War II as well as a long and brutal occupation by the Japanese. Now Communist forces from the north were hurling themselves in their direction, bringing unspeakable violence and certain death to thousands upon thousands of innocent men, women, and children unfortunate enough to end up in their sights. These exhausted nurses were vulnerable to the terror that even now moved closer and closer with each passing minute. There was no world power to snatch them away to safety, no well-equipped, modern army to halt the aggressor bearing down on them. They lay exposed, directly in the path of destruction, and there was nothing she could do about it.

With a final glance back at the moonlit structures dotting the medical compound, Grace picked up her suitcase and joined the other Americans heading for the city.

Finally, when all foreign families were accounted for, the long convoy headed out from the Embassy motor pool and began its journey through the chaotic streets toward Inchon harbor. The collection of 608 women and children included United States government employees as well as families from various mission groups.

The line of vehicles stopped at Ascom City about twenty miles southwest of Seoul, where everyone was herded into a large concrete building at the headquarters of the American Military Advisory Group. Russian-made Yak fighters roared by overhead every now and then, looking for targets of opportunity to strafe into oblivion.

After downing a breakfast and lunch of U.S. Army rations, the group was waiting for further orders when a member of the American Embassy came up to Grace and said, "Mrs. Rue, would you please accompany me to the seaport at Inchon?"

"Whatever you say," the woman replied, assuming that the authorities wanted her for some medical emergency.

When they arrived at the seaport, Grace saw a very disturbed woman strapped to a stretcher. She started to lend assistance when the embassy staff member called, "No, Mrs. Rue. We have something else for you to do. We will take care of her."

"What is it you want from me?" Grace asked.

The man pointed at a large freighter waiting nearby. "We're sending the women and children out on that," he announced, "and we'd like for you to organize the people as they're brought on board. There are a few staterooms available for those who are ill, pregnant, or with very small children." The man turned to his companion, a look of frustration shadowing his face. "We originally had two ships standing by, but this is the only one we could make ready for the voyage in such short notice. Anything you could do to help us would be greatly appreciated."

Grace nodded. "I'll be happy to assist you in any way I can. Let me check things out and make arrangements for our special-needs passengers."

Crewmen on the Norwegian commercial fertilizer freighter *Reinhold* had hurriedly swept the ship's cavernous hold as clean as possible, trying desperately to make it ready to receive a far more precious cargo than it had ever carried. American Ambassador John Muccio had pressed the ship into service.

Grace evaluated the vessel from bow to stern, examining the sparse accommodations, making sure that everyone would have a place to settle in once the convoy arrived from Ascom City. Freighters such as this one were home to rough, seagoing laborers and tons of sometimes-toxic cargo—not women and children running from a war.

On board, she found a mess hall and twelve cabins. As the evacuees stumbled up the gangplank, she assigned two pregnant women, both close to delivery, to two of the cabins. Mothers with babies and small children filled the others. Six hundred and eighty passengers jammed themselves onto a ship that usually accommodated twelve.

Because the hold was crowded and stuffy, some of the women chose to stay on the main deck housed in several tents. Grace accepted full responsibility for all passengers, working amid the panic that any such activity within a war-zone generates. Fully armed North Korean warplanes circled overhead from time to time, then moved on, their pilots apparently deciding that sinking a boatload of fleeing foreign women and children would do nothing to advance the war effort.

On deck, the scene was anything but tranquil. One woman, an alcoholic, had to be tied down to keep her from falling overboard. "How could I explain to your husband if we lose you?" Grace asked her, trying to keep her from fighting the ropes.

Yet another woman went completely out of control as she began experiencing withdrawal from the drugs with which her husband regularly injected her. Her violence made her a danger to herself and others. Eventually, Grace had three women tied down securely for their own safety.

On Monday, June 26, 1950, the *Reinhold* and its accompanying American destroyer slipped out of Inchon harbor and headed for Japan, leaving behind a dock filled with worried husbands who would be flown out of the country as soon as transport could be made available. The remaining men didn't have long to wait. News reached them at midnight that it was time for them to head to the airport as quickly as they could.

Dr. John Scharffenberg, a 1948 graduate of the College of Medical Evangelists and a member of the Seoul Sanitarium and Hospital team, remembers the journey as very, very frightening. Writing for the CME *Alumni Journal* several months later, he reported, "One of the Americans became sick with polio and died Tuesday morning. We had to leave without even burying him.

"We could see the North Korean and South Korean planes fighting overhead. En route to the airport, our convoy was strafed several times. I recall seeing a Korean right across the street from us hit by one of the strafing planes. Blood gushed from his abdomen and dripped down both legs, but he was still on his feet, and several friends were helping him into a jeep to take him to a hospital.

"Just before leaving the Kimpo airport we received a telephone call from our folks at the hospital, and they said the North Koreans were shelling the hospital with mortars. Since then we have received no word and do not know how much has been damaged. We understand that 300 to 400 city officials were executed the day after the North Koreans came in.

"As [the plane sent to evacuate us] was attempting to land, several North Korean planes were attacking the Kimpo airdrome, but the American [escort fighters] shot them down. Even after we had taken off, another plane came in to attack us, but it was shot down. I understand some bullets went through some parts of [our] plane."

The flight to Japan took two hours, and the men arrived just before the ship carrying their families docked. During the sea journey aboard the *Reinhold*, the eight-month-old daughter of mission dentist Mead Baldwin developed a high fever as did four-month-old Charles Mills, the youngest son of Robert Mills, treasurer of the Korean Union Mission. Both infants were rushed to American Army hospitals, where they remained in critical condition for some time before finally being released. Several adults from the ship became ill as well.

When medical authorities determined that the Baldwin girl was suffering from smallpox, they attempted to contact all the dispersed passengers and determine whether they had been inoculated for the disease.

Doctor Rue's son-in-law, Leland Mitchell, and daughter, Betty, with baby Barbara in her arms, left Japan the very next day for America. Later in the week, Grace climbed aboard a San Francisco-bound airliner and joined a very thankful and relieved George just in time for the start of the General Conference session.

But, while the Rues were being blessed by the meetings and inspiring reports from Church delegates gathered from around the world, the situation in Seoul deteriorated completely. Those hardworking and dedicated nurses Grace had left sleeping in their beds, along with the other personnel who were fighting day and night to keep the hospital open, faced the most terrifying days of their lives. Some would survive the storm. Some would not.

Children of
God

Dr. Chung Sa Young, assistant director of the
Seoul Sanitarium and Hospital, looked out over the
grim faces staring back at him. In the distance, exploding
shells and the rattle of machinegun fire disturbed the morning stillness.
Doctor Rue was gone. Grace Rue was gone. Miss Robson, the hospital's
director of nursing services, was gone. The American presence that, for
the past few years, had offered professional guidance as well as spiritual
and financial support for the medical work in Korea, had been whisked
away. All that remained was a frightened staff of men and women who
were about to face an enemy of almost limitless power and resources.

Each person in that gathering knew the South Korean Cavalry was
engaged in battle with the advancing Communist army not too many
miles from where they sat. Men on horseback were defending their country against men in tanks. The thought sickened them.

"I'm requesting that as many of you as possible stay on campus to
help guard the hospital," Dr. Young stated, trying to control his emotions. "However, first- and second-year students should leave immediately. We've all heard the reports from northern refugees. We know what
our enemy is capable of doing to those who stand in their way. However, we serve a God who will have the final say in this crisis. He's more
powerful than any army or ideology. What happens to us today or to-

morrow isn't as important as what will happen to us when Jesus comes. Evil may take our bodies, but it can't steal our eternity. No matter how you choose to face the enemy, no matter what he does to you, our loving God will win the final battle."

Heads nodded in agreement as soft sobs echoed throughout the room. Suddenly a voice called angrily from the back of the assembly. "Why? Why are the North Koreans attacking us?"

Dr. Chung sighed. "From what I've learned, the United States recently moved its seventh fleet into the Formosa Strait in order to protect the flank of American forces in the area and prevent the island of Formosa from falling into Communist hands. The government of the People's Republic of China interpreted this action as a threat to the Chinese mainland, and so they launched the invasion across the thirty-eighth parallel. They figure that our South Korean Army can be easily defeated and that American occupation forces have been softened by the lack of action in our country. From the speed with which their army is moving, it seems they're right on both counts.

"So," the speaker continued, "I'm asking you to dismiss all patients and send them home, leaving only the very critically ill. Last night, while a group of us were gathered in the campus church praying and reciting the twenty-third psalm, we heard a terrible explosion. We've since learned that it was the Joong Ryang River Bridge being blown up. If your home is on the other side of that river, you'll have to do some swimming. My advice to those of you who leave is to head south as quickly as you can. Don't wait another minute. Go now, and may God go with you."

Within the hour, the hospital campus was like a ghost town with a greatly reduced staff caring for the few remaining patients who were too weak or too ill to be moved. One of those who stayed behind was Miss Verna Pak, a senior nursing student. Her instructor, Grace Ahn, assigned her to the TB unit. By Wednesday morning, she could hear the *ratta-tat-tat* of machine guns and the percussive *thump, thump, thump* of exploding bombs coming from the direction of the city. She went about her duties with one eye focused on the front entrance of the unit, totally expecting the appearance of crazed soldiers in blood-caked boots and drawn bayonets.

Around noon, it suddenly became very quiet. There wasn't a sound anywhere.

A staff member burst into the room, causing Verna to jump in fear. "They've taken Seoul!" he announced. "I heard it on the radio. The North Koreans have occupied the center of the city." The man began to pace. "That means the Americans will be counterattacking just six miles from here. Six miles! Artillery shells can travel farther than that! And if the downtown area has been destroyed, we will be the only hospital left standing to treat the injured. Do you know what that means?"

"What?"

"That means our beds will soon be filled with Communist soldiers. That means that we may have to save the lives of the very men who murdered our fathers, brothers, wives, or children."

"No!" Verna said, lifting her hand. "We will *not* be treating Communists soldiers or murderers in this hospital. We will be treating children of God; our brothers and sisters in Christ. Doctors and nurses must never refuse treatment to anyone because of who they are or what they may have done. This is a Seventh-day Adventist hospital; a *Christian* institution. We treat everyone the same. Everyone!"

Her companion nodded slowly, his fear and anger subsiding. "That's what Doctor Rue taught us," he said, tears spilling down his pale cheeks. "He told us that God loves us no matter how sinful we are, and that we must love others the same way He loves us. I . . . I just don't know if I can do it, Verna. I just don't know."

Miss Pak turned back to her work. "We can, and we will," she said quietly.

Three hours later, the afternoon silence was shattered by the high-pitched scream of American fighter planes as they attacked North Korean positions along the Joong Ryang River, less than a mile from the campus. That night injured and dying Communist soldiers began arriving at the hospital.

The North Korean forces not only withstood the American fighter assault but continued their march southward, leaving a devastated city in their wake. Civilians, running for their lives, had to abandon sick or enfeebled relatives. Mothers with babies strapped to their backs felt their precious cargoes grow limp as shrapnel from bursting bombs whistled around them. With no time to stop, they simply unfastened the cords and let the now-silent bundles fall to the ground.

A few days later, Communist officers rounded up thirty of the hospital's remaining staff and student nurses, including Verna Pak, and shipped them by night to the 24th and 25th North Korean Evacuation Hospitals. The group was divided into teams with one nurse and one doctor to care for about forty patients. The man who was assigned to be the doctor for Miss Pak's team was, in reality, a medical student with only three months of training. Verna had to show him how to change the dressing of soldiers with shrapnel wounds.

As North Korean hospitals filled to overflowing, nurses were instructed to perform their rounds in nearby homes, factories, and schools to care for the endless stream of wounded. Food and medical supplies ran low, but the burned and maimed continued to pour in unabated.

Before long, Verna found herself working near the town of Taejon. "There's a Seventh-day Adventist church here," she said to herself as she ended her shift one evening. Arriving at the pastor's home in search of safe lodging, she discovered that eleven other nurses had taken refuge there as well. One had shown up at the front door with a bag of rice strapped to her back. For ten days, the group kept themselves alive and on the job using the energy provided by that single bag of rice.

One day, they heard the *boom, boom, BOOM* of heavy artillery. Taejon was under attack! The nurses, along with the pastor and his family, escaped to a small mountain cottage hidden in a wooded area at the edge of town. The structure was too small to hold everyone at once, so the frightened fugitives took turns sleeping outside as screaming artillery shells raced overhead and slammed into the ground nearby. Explosions filled the air with the acrid stench of burning munitions and scorched flesh.

When the firefight stopped, the group stumbled back through the rubble to the pastor's house.

In one month alone, the now reenergized Allies flew nearly 30,000 sorties, showering the Communist forces with airborne death and destruction. By the end of August, the daytime air attacks on North Korean armor and troop concentrations combined with the nighttime harassment of their supply columns and the deadly B-29 carpet bombing of their scattered ranks, began pushing the invaders back the way they'd come. When American victories blunted their offensive near the Pusan Perimeter, the Communist offensive crumbled.

On August 31, the North mounted a last desperate attempt to defeat the defenders. For a short while, it appeared that the North Koreans would break through. But their lack of an effective air power and the close and very efficient support of the United States Air Force, Marine Corps Aviation, and the Royal Australian Air Force, together with valiant fighting by the United States and Republic of Korea ground forces, gradually exhausted the enemy beyond recovery. Allied forces broke out of the Pusan Perimeter and marched north, pushing the invaders ahead of them.

On September 15, 1950, United States general Douglas MacArthur and his United Nations troops made a daring amphibious landing at Inchon, about a hundred miles below the thirty-eighth parallel, in line with Seoul and some 165 miles behind North Korean lines. The Inchon beachhead had been softened up by two days of naval and air bombardment, and the attack was supported by a multi-national fleet of 262 ships, including the U.S. battleship *Missouri,* which blasted away with her sixteen-inch guns from the Sea of Japan. The assault was a bold turning point. Lives lost in that action included 536 Americans and between 30,000 and 40,000 North Koreans.

The United Nations Command recaptured Seoul on September 26 and cut the North Korean lines in half. As the enemy grew disorganized and defeated, the Allies took 125,000 captives, seized the North Korean capital, Pyongyang, and forced the Communists all the way back to the Yalu River on the border with China.

The Communist Evacuation hospital where Miss Pak worked suddenly became a United Nations hospital, and its patients prisoners of war. Miss Pak offered to continue her work in the operating room because she had much experience there.

The first day after the facility changed hands, a patient was admitted with a seriously injured and infected leg. His condition deteriorated so badly that the limb needed to be amputated. During the procedure, the patient began to bleed uncontrollably, and the doctor in charge tried to stop the flow by clamping off the vein. But the bleeding continued. Miss Pak quickly applied a tourniquet and saved the man's life.

"Good job!" the doctor said, wiping his forehead with the back of his bloodstained hand. "Where did you learn to work so quickly?"

"At the Seoul Sanitarium and Hospital," Miss Pak stated proudly as she secured the tourniquet and began wiping away the spilled blood.

"You're a very good nurse," the doctor said.

"I had very good teachers," Verna responded humbly.

The next day, a South Korean policeman appeared at the hospital and demanded that Miss Pak and her colleague, Sunny Whang, follow him to the police station.

"Why are you taking us away from our work?" they asked as they were bodily shoved through the front door and out onto the street.

"You've helped North Korean soldiers!" the man shouted angrily. "You've given aid and comfort to our enemy. That's against the law. You will be dealt with accordingly."

As they approached the man's car, an American Military Police jeep drove up, and the two nurses broke away from their angry captor and ran to the driver. "Help us," they cried in Korean. "They are going to kill us for being traitors. But we aren't traitors. We're Christian nurses who'll treat anyone who's sick or injured."

The big American soldier frowned, not understanding a word the women were saying. But he could see the desperation in their eyes. He also noticed their worn and stained nurse's uniforms and began to realize that whatever was making the policeman so angry probably wasn't their fault.

"Don't go with him," he warned.

The policeman ran up to the MP and pointed at the two women. "Soviet, Soviet!" he shouted, trying to make the man believe that the two nurses were Communists. The American ignored him.

With a final scowl and a few choice words only the women could understand, the policeman turned on his heel and stormed away.

Thinking that the constable would return, the two nurses, along with four others at the pastor's home, decided to stay away from the hospital for a few days. Eventually, the call to duty became so strong that they returned. But the policeman who'd attempted to arrest them hadn't given up. On their way back to work, the nurses were captured and taken to a police station and forced to kneel on the hard, cement floor of their cell.

That evening, a stern-faced officer appeared at the bars. Unlocking the door to their cell he ordered, "Seoul Sanitarium Hospital nurses, follow me." *This is it,* the nurses said silently to themselves. *We're going to be killed.*

In the next room, the assistant police chief stood to his feet and walked over to the group. Then, he bowed. "I'm sorry," he said softly. "You're simply nurses doing your jobs. We were wrong to arrest and detain you. The people of South Korea appreciate your dedication and hard work. You're free to go home."

And go home they did. In mid-October 1950, the nurses returned to the Seoul Sanitarium and Hospital and took up their duties once again, working with civilian patients and praising God for His love and care.

On the other side of the world, George and Grace Rue stood before an official of their own government who sat shaking her head slowly from side to side. "We're not issuing visas to anyone for Korea at this time," she said flatly.

George leaned forward slightly. "The United States ambassador to Korea has made an official request through the Seventh-day Adventist Mission Board. The situation in Seoul has stabilized. President Rhee has personally asked that my wife and I be allowed to return immediately."

The woman behind the desk gasped. "You're *that* Doctor George Rue?"

"Yes. And this is my wife, Grace."

"Oh, there was a slight misunderstanding, Doctor Rue," she announced apologetically, flipping through the visitors' passports and applying a stamp to a selected page in each. "Your names had already been approved. Sorry for the delay."

George and Grace thankfully gathered up their documents and left the building, their minds filled with plans for their return to Korea. What had taken five months in 1947 had taken only minutes in 1950!

The Rues arrived in Tokyo on October 15 after being in the air for thirty hours. Military officials instructed them to be at the airport before 9:00 A.M. the following day.

Bright and early the next morning, suitcases in hand, they waited as a large Douglas DC-4 rolled up to their gate, engines running. On its nose was painted the word *Bataan*, and on its tail appeared five stars. The aircraft belonged to General Douglas MacArthur, who'd just returned from Wake Island, where he'd met with a worried and somewhat unhappy President Truman. The president didn't appreciate MacArthur's aggressive plans for handling the politically charged situation in North Korea and told him so in no uncertain terms.

When the aircraft landed at Kimpo, the passengers, including returning American Ambassador Muccio, who had been with MacArthur on Wake, noted with great sadness that the hangars were but bare skeletons, and the terminal lay in total ruin. While overjoyed to be back, the Rues were overwhelmed by the devastation. Even from the air they could see that the countryside was littered with bomb craters, damaged and burned-out tanks, trucks, jeeps, and artillery pieces.

An American Army officer offered to take George and Grace to the hospital compound in his jeep. Seoul had been 70 percent destroyed. The shells of buildings stood as silent testimony to the violence that had befallen the capital and its proud people. Retreating Communist soldiers had started most of the fires that consumed the city. Every bridge across the Han River was now only a collection of twisted, unusable steel. One-way pontoon bridges did their best to handle the traffic jamming every road.

Along the way, the new arrivals could see cleanup crews at work and other teams of laborers attempting to repair the electrical and telephone lines throughout the metropolis.

Doctor Rue and Grace arrived at the Seoul Sanitarium and Hospital about 3:30 P.M. Later, writing of the experience in the *Alumni Journal,* George stated, "It was a real homecoming. We did not know who we would see, who'd been killed, or who were still missing. How good it was to see these people who had been through so much. They came running from everywhere. It's impossible to express our emotions.

"All of our folks are thin, hungry looking, and poorly clothed. They've lost everything or have sold all they had to get a little something to eat, for they have had no income of any sort for over four months.

"Many of the staff spent weeks at a time in the hills, moving about from night to night and living on next to nothing. Three church members hid out in a chicken house. Many were listed to be shot. Only five are known to be dead, though many are still missing."

The Rues found that the hospital, school, and other properties had not suffered significant damage, although several bombs had leveled homes and part of the office building on the Korean Union Mission compound. Allied forces coming over the hills behind the hospital had surprised the Communist soldiers, forcing them into retreat before they had time to completely destroy the facilities.

The North Korean Army had conscripted several hospital employees and taken captive others, including the nurses.

As they beat their hasty retreat, the Communists had taken whatever medical supplies and surgical instruments they could carry. Dental equipment, wrapped for departure, had been left behind.

While some windows had been shattered, the hospital building itself was in good condition. A high-ranking North Korean officer, who'd been a patient there before the war and held Dr. Rue in high esteem, ordered the building spared.

In January 1951, Doctor Rue estimated that it would take approximately $100,000 to put things in shape again, including necessary equipment, labor, and materials. He shared with friends a comment made by a non-Christian businessman who visited the area soon after their return. "Your God surely has protected your people and your property," the man said with a shake of his head.

George had responded, "It surely is true when one drives through Seoul and sees all that has come to this large city, and then sees our property. We can see how the Lord has blessed us."

Grace discovered that their house had been emptied. Fortunately, hospital personnel had hidden the Rue's cooking utensils, bedding, furniture, and personal clothing before the Communists arrived. The couple looked around and found an old piece of carpet out in the grass all covered with weeds. They threw it over some box springs, and that's where they slept. Soldiers, including North Koreans, had occupied their beautiful home while they were away.

Soon, the hospital filled with patients. But, this time, the beds contained many injured children. Every time the battle lines had changed, countless civilian casualties resulted. Thousands of children, including infants, had lost one or both parents. Grace took special notice of this new phenomenon of war, welcoming each child with open arms and all the love she could spare.

She and George had returned with a tenacious belief that they could help heal the souls and bodies of men, women, and children under the shifting darkness of war. They rose to the challenge of revitalizing the Seventh-day Adventist medical work in Korea. And, in giving, received.

In a letter to *The Medical Evangelist,* Doctor Rue told of even greater opportunities opening before them and shared his growing respect for his Korean colleagues. "Our people have been through great trial and have been strengthened by it," he wrote. "They've come out with a new vision of what they need in their own lives and what needs to be done in the work before the Lord comes. I have been greatly encouraged as I have talked with them and hope the missionaries who return can match their vision and zeal."

But, what was perceived as the end of the Korean War, was just an enticing interval. An even greater storm waited to be unleashed on the country. This time, George and Grace wouldn't be on the outside looking in. In a matter of weeks, they'd find themselves standing at the very center of the tempest.

Get Out Now!

News broadcasts, stirring the airwaves throughout the world, began to carry ominous messages as the coldest winter in Korea's history tightened its grip on the devastated land. Allied forces, under the direction of General Douglas MacArthur, had pushed the Communists north of the thirty-eighth parallel and seemed to be headed straight for the Yula River, North Korea's boundary with China. Just on the other side of that river waited a nation with 300,000 well-armed and well-trained troops prepared to push back. "The presence of UN troops in North Korea is unacceptable to the security of the People's Republic of China," government officials warned. Their words fell on deaf ears.

In November, six Russian-made Mig-15s roared across the Yula and attacked a flight of World War II vintage P-51 Mustangs flown by a group of very outclassed American airmen. Behind the Migs marched those 300,000 troops determined to finish what their North Korean comrades had failed to do—capture South Korea and rid the country of its bothersome UN presence.

Within three weeks, the Communists had driven Allied forces back across the thirty-eighth parallel. Their advance was slowed temporarily by the appearance of newly minted F-86 Sabre jets with stars and stripes painted on their wings. The United States was letting China know that they, too, were capable of building fighter jets.

In December, the Communists regrouped and headed south once again.

News of the approaching army filled the staff at the Seoul Sanitarium and Hospital with a cold uneasiness. This time there was added fuel to ignite their fear. Word had raced throughout the country that the North Koreans and their Chinese allies were planning to execute all the Christians they found. George realized that the only way to save the people who worked under him was to make arrangements for as many of them as possible to join the mammoth migration of refugees streaming south toward Pusan, South Korea's second largest city. This coastal municipality, facing the Korea Straits two hundred and seventy miles from Seoul, would be their only hope for survival. The man in charge of the U.S. Embassy motor pool would let George know how much space was available for people and supplies in embassy cars and boats. "We have room for eight people and twelve boxes of equipment," he'd say over the phone. "Fill it!"

Freight cars heading south were jammed to overflowing. Fearful passengers clung to the top of swaying boxcars, fighting winds of thirty degrees below zero and the constant danger of debilitating frostbite. Snow squalls limited mobility and visibility. Thousands feared falling asleep lest they freeze. Many lost their grip on the vibrating, jolting cars and slipped to their death.

Tucked in corners or stacked in overhead compartments or storage bins rode a steady flow of hospital supplies, heading for a new place of service, ready to aid doctors and nurses in the desperate business of saving lives uprooted by war.

In the battle zones, canteens froze. Perspiration in boots and on beards turned to ice. Many guns had to be fired every half-hour to keep their internal lubrication solvent. Soldiers on both sides burned whatever they could find including household goods, doors, and flooring in an attempt to keep warm.

Finally, as 1950 drew to a close, only George, Grace, Miss Robson, and fifteen hospital employees remained on campus. George's worst fears had not been realized. He, with the help of the God he loved, had managed to send his entire workforce south, out of harm's way.

Lieutenant General Matthew Bunker Ridgway, field commander of the Allied forces in Korea, had 365,000 men dug in just south of the thirty-eighth parallel waiting for the Northern forces—now 500,000 strong with one million Manchurian soldiers in reserve—to make their move. On New Year's Day, 1951, they did.

By mid-afternoon, combat casualties started arriving at the hospital. Simultaneously, word reached George from the United States Embassy. "Get out," the message stated. "Get out NOW!"

The next morning, the last flight from Seoul's Kimpo Airport carried Grace and Miss Robson on their way to Pusan, leaving George and his small staff to close up shop. With the percussive sounds of heavy artillery echoing through the frigid air, Doctor Rue and his companions did their best to prepare the campus for what was to come. George told the attendant in the boiler room to open the valve and drain the heating system when he left. Windows were boarded up and what medical valuables remained were quickly stored.

The following day, American Shooting Stars and Hellcats screamed overhead, providing air support for the struggling front lines. That afternoon, the American ambassador let George know that an American convoy was being readied and that he should have his fifteen remaining workers and himself safely packed in the hospital's jeep and three-quarter-ton truck and in town as soon as possible. Special papers and windshield stickers would be provided, giving them clearance to cross the military pontoon bridge over the Han River just south of Seoul.

Realizing that he could carry more people in the truck, George immediately contacted a dozen Koreans and told them to be ready to leave with the hospital staff. He hurried to the Adventist college five miles distant to check on its status. Along the way he saw soldiers sitting around campfires, reminding him of paintings he'd seen of George Washington's army at Valley Forge.

Only a handful of people remained at the college, and they were busy carrying out school equipment and supplies, items he knew they'd use later to barter for food. He asked a man rushing by how the students and faculty had planned to evade the approaching army. "They went away," came the hurried reply.

"How?" George asked, running to keep up with the frightened Korean. "The trains are full, and there are no airplanes flying."

The man pointed south. "They walk."

"To Pusan?" Doctor Rue gasped. "That's over two-hundred miles away!"

"They take cattle for milk, and they walk." With that, the man stumbled on down the road, a family of his own to protect.

At exactly 5:45 P.M. George started his journey alone, steering his vehicle through the panic-filled streets to the Han River where he joined the convoy parked near the pontoon bridge.

The waterway was choked with huge cakes of floating ice that, at any moment, could damage the pontoons holding up the only roadway to safety. One hundred thousand troops with heavy equipment including British Centurion tanks and American eight-inch howitzer artillery pieces jammed the streets. Fearing that the growing throng of refugees might overwhelm the bridge and the city's military presence, General Ridgway ordered his military police to fire over the heads of civilians that refused to stay out of the way. If they didn't, the soldiers had orders to shoot them dead on the spot.

Five footbridges provided a somewhat shaky escape route for the exodus; in places, refugees had to walk across the frozen river. Hundreds of thousands, some barefoot and half-clothed, carrying or dragging whatever personal belongings they could, made their way through the darkness. Mothers tugged at shivering children. Old men, bent over by tremendous loads lashed to their backs, shuffled through the snow, some leaving bright red stains in their tracks.

The embassy vehicles finally crossed the Han River around ten o'clock that night. Like a captain leaving a sinking ship, George was the last in his group to make the dangerous portage. At six o'clock the next morning, North Korea re-took Seoul.

The convoy reached Pusan the evening of Thursday, January 4. George quickly located Grace and Miss Robson at the nurses' barracks at a local evacuation hospital and then drove to the military officers' mess seven miles away to get something to eat and find a place to stay.

All persons eating at the officers' mess had to register and indicate their units. A weary Doctor Rue signed his name and wrote, "SDA" after it. Because Seventh-day Adventists enjoyed a good reputation throughout the country, no one questioned him.

Pusan, a town of 250,000, had been transformed. More than two million frightened, exhausted, and grieving refugees crowded its streets, all in need of food and some form of shelter from the unrelenting cold. Men, women, and children searched the throngs for lost loved ones, hoping against hope that the war had left them untouched. Thousands never found those they looked for.

A few days later, George's and Grace's hearts sang for joy as they welcomed Verna Pak and her group of students to the city. The tired travelers reported, with great agony of spirit, that when they left Seoul, only the very old or recently orphaned remained, those least likely to survive the violent occupation sweeping down upon them. The rag-tag group from the college with their life-saving herd of cows eventually stumbled into town as well without the loss of one!

From Pusan, foreigners were being evacuated out of the country, some to the Philippines, others to Hawaii. But George and his group remained. The recently arrived hospital staff and other church members, numbering around 1,100, crowded into two small churches and a large tent. People spread rice mats across the floor, end to end, doing their best to get a good night's sleep. Some even tried to spend the night sitting up.

Everyone was scared, and for good reason. Pusan was safe. But how long would that last? Behind them raced the North Korean army, their progress being slowed by hard-fighting Allied forces. In front of them waited the cold Sea of Japan. They felt like the Children of Israel standing at the Red Sea as Pharaoh and his forces thundered in their direction.

One evening, while eating supper at the mess hall, George overheard two officers talking. He leaned forward, trying to hear above the din of military personnel and the clatter of dishes. "I just came from Cheju Island," he heard one say, speaking of a piece of fertile volcanic land jutting out of the Yellow Sea seventy-five miles southwest of the Korean peninsula. "The place is in pretty bad shape. What bothers me the most is the total lack of medical help for the refugees. Those people are really suffering. They need doctors and nurses, and they need them now!"

George cleared his throat and caught the two men's attention. "Excuse me," he said. "My name is Doctor Rue, and I think I can give you all the help you need!"

George immediately contacted his church leaders exiled in Japan. Soon, Robert Mills, Korean Union Mission treasurer, and Union President E.W. Bahr flew to Pusan to see what arrangements could be made to respond to the situation on Cheju as well as find a safer haven for the Adventist workers crowded into the city.

George and Robert Mills negotiated with the United States attaché for a LST—a military vessel designed to transport tanks, bulldozers, road-building equipment, heavy artillery, and general cargo—to carry the workers to the island.

Word of this new exodus spread quickly among the exiled missionaries of all faiths. When the ship docked, an eager group of 5,000 passengers composed of Seventh-day Adventists, Presbyterians, Methodists, and other denominations waited to climb on board.

George ran out on the street and started directing traffic as Grace identified those who clamored up the gangplank. She wanted to make sure that the entire hospital staff and all of the Adventist workers were safely on board. Then, one by one, other passengers pressed themselves into the large hold, crew cabins, and walkways of the vessel until all were tucked in securely. George even convinced the hesitant ship officials to allow the hospital jeep and truck to be included on the manifest. As the ship set sail, other vessels docked in its wake ready to receive more refugees.

During the two-day voyage on the LST, two babies were born, and two elderly people passed away.

Mills and Bahr flew to Cheju ahead of the ship and purchased two large bags of rice and then made arrangements for several families on the island to prepare a huge meal. When the boat arrived, every passenger on board found a hot, steaming bowl of rice waiting for him or her!

Doctor Clarence Lee and others from the sanitarium established an outpatient clinic at a Ko Sung school on the northeast corner of the island and began seeing as many as 300 patients a day. Hospital workers didn't have beds to call their own, but they felt fortunate to find at their disposal an even greater luxury. A bathtub!

The ever-industrious Miss Robson quickly launched an outreach program to help serve the quarter million refugees crowded onto the island. She organized her Korean nurses into groups and began visiting refugee camps and villages to administer inoculations for typhoid, cholera, and the deadly smallpox germ to those at risk. While no one counted the number of inoculations given, estimates reach into the thousands.

Shortly after their arrival on Cheju, Central Intelligence Agency personnel began checking all the names of those who had been on board the LST, searching for Communist sympathizers. Two names jumped out at them. Verna Pak and Sunny Whang. The man in charge of the operation called for the captain on his staff. Pointing at a sheet of paper he said, "We have a report that these two women, nurses, were captured and held in North Korea for providing medical services to Communist soldiers." Looking up he said coldly, "Find them."

The captain lost no time in tracking down the two women. As Verna and Sunny stood facing him in his office, they felt like history was trying to repeat itself. "Yes, we treated North Korean soldiers," they admitted. "When they were brought in with their bodies torn apart, we didn't ask for which government they worked. Most were half-dead and couldn't have answered if they'd tried. But we saved their lives not because we're Communist sympathizers but because we're nurses. Not only that, we're *Christian* nurses. And we've also taken the Nightingale pledge to help sick people regardless of who they are. If you were close to death, would you want us to be asking you to explain your allegiances before we administered medical assistance? Or would you want us to help save your life?"

The captain nodded. "You're right, of course. This war makes everyone a little suspicious. I'm just doing my job."

The women bowed in respect and responded. "Yes, captain. And we're just doing ours."

A few months later, that same CIA operative became very sick and was brought to a clinic for medical attention. Who should receive him warmly and nurse him back to health but Verna Pak and Sunny Whang. Not once did they ask him under which government he served.

Local newspaper and radio reports told of the fierce fighting raging to the north. Communist and Allied forces remained locked in deadly conflict, suffering terrible losses at each other's hands as well as succumbing to the bipartisan attack of horrible winter weather.

Soon after the Rues arrived in Pusan, a story reported by both radio and newspapers centered on a woman who'd given birth under a bridge. President Rhee's wife, living in exile with her husband in the city, sent a driver to find Grace in order to ask her directly whether her husband could do something to prevent this kind of thing from ever happening again. Grace responded by saying that George had not been able to find a suitable structure in Pusan in which to establish any kind of medical work. "But," she added, "we will find a place."

In a matter of days, Grace received another message, this time from the mayor of Pusan. "Mrs. Rhee has asked me to provide a building for you to use," he wrote. "We've discovered three that may or may not be suitable. Please come and inspect them at your earliest convenience."

George soon selected an official site for the Pusan branch of the Seoul Sanitarium and Hospital. "It's an old barn," he told the staff on his return, "with one large room measuring seventeen by twenty-four feet. I believe we can accommodate around twenty adult patients." He smiled apologetically. "It isn't much, but it's the best we can do under the circumstances."

When the hospital workers arrived in Pusan, suitcases in hand, they found that the building George had described had one added feature he'd failed to mention. The facility in which they were to do battle with injury, disease, and germs boasted a partial dirt floor. However, it did offer shelter from the snow and wind, so what the floor lacked, the rest of the structure made up for with its sturdy walls and reasonably secure roof.

An X-ray unit and laboratory were quickly set up using equipment brought down in the truck. Even with a dire lack of medicines and other pharmaceuticals, the Rues opened their doors for business. Nurses not only worked in shifts, they slept in shifts, using the meager accommodations.

Writing to friends in America, George praised his staff unrestrainedly. "Many of them have lost every personal possession, and many have lost relatives. But, in spite of all the loss and extreme suffering they have gone through, one hears very little complaining. It's remarkable! It's impossible for me to describe the picture here. You'd have to see it to believe it. All these people own are the few items they managed to carry with them out of the North. But, their courage is strong, and they're thankful to the Lord for sparing their lives. Surely the Lord has cared for His people in this terrible time, and He has delivered them."

Establishing a hospital in Pusan, even one in a barn, was the easy part. Finding housing for the staff presented a major challenge. A few workers found shelter in some tiny huts, measuring six feet by six feet, behind the hospital. Four couples, some with children, set up house-keeping in a fifteen-by-thirty-foot tent divided into four "apartments" using curtains. The boys and some of the married couples set up tents on wooden platforms bridging a sewage ditch. This particular group had even more reason to hope that the war would end before the spring thaw.

Conditions in the hospital itself were little better. There was no wait-ing room. People needing medical care either stood in the hallway en-trance or waited out on the street. When patients met their doctors, it was in small offices furnished with benches, examining tables, chairs, and desks made from packing crates. Curtain partitions fashioned from bed sheets separated the X-ray room, laboratory, and pharmacy from the twenty-bed ward. Instruments had to be sanitized in a pressure ster-ilizer sitting over a charcoal fire. A pot-bellied stove did its best to pro-vide a semblance of heat. Maternity and emergency cases made up for most of the 250 patients a day that streamed through the facility.

Doctor Rue performed emergency-only surgery on an old surgery table using a portable sterilizer, a bathroom for scrubbing in, and a totally inadequate supply of instruments. Once while attempting a ce-sarean-section delivery on a woman who'd walked two miles for help, the electricity powering his little electric heater blinked off. The chilling ten-degree air outside soon began penetrating the thin operating room walls. George prayed that he'd be given enough strength to complete the procedure and that God would keep his fingers from going numb.

As he feverishly worked within the cavity, he discovered something he'd never experienced before. In such adverse circumstances, the inside of a patient is a lot warmer than the outside air. As long as his hands remained on the job, cutting, sewing, and manipulating the tissue opened before him, his fingers remained warm enough to work. He placed his last stitch almost an hour later, thankful that his patient had unknowingly given as much as she had received.

Maternity cases constituted much of the work. In time, Doctor Rue and his staff would deliver 3,500 babies in what everyone affectionately called "The Old Barn."

Friend Mildred Watts, writing from Kansas City where husband Ralph served as president of the Missouri Conference, acknowledged the wonderful work George and Grace were doing in their makeshift "branch" of the Seoul hospital. "I know that your very presence among the Koreans will help their morale," she wrote in a much-appreciated letter. "They are certainly facing a Gethsemane. George, I want to assure you that we all think of you and pray for you, and we admire the spirit of sacrifice and service which has been activating you since the time you first accepted the call to go to Korea as a medical missionary."

Doctor Rue, always quick to share accolades sent in his direction, responded to the letter with one of his own. "Grace and Irene Robson have been invaluable," he reported. "By their very presence they've given courage to our people and have been hard at work everyday. At no time have they ever complained in any way and, as far as I know, have they ever been afraid. Now, with our medical work on Cheju and here in Pusan, and with Seoul opening up soon, their presence and help will be more appreciated than ever."

One day while George was walking along the crowded streets of Pusan, he saw a gentleman leading a cow by a length of rope. It was obvious that the animal had recently gone head-to-head with a barbed wire fence and that the fence had won.

George told the worried farmer to stay where he was. A few minutes later, the doctor returned with some instruments and two nurses in tow. There, on the street, surrounded by curious onlookers, George Rue and his medical team treated the injured cow. The good doctor fully understood that the animal might well be the farmer's only earthly possession and that it was more than likely his family's only source of milk. By treating the cow, George was in fact treating the farmer's entire family.

On January 25, 1951, General Ridgway launched what he called "Operation Thunderbolt," the successful and methodical advance of UN forces toward Seoul, fully exploiting their superiority in artillery, armor, and air power. The Chinese vigorously contested the operation until February 9, when they suddenly and inexplicably retreated. Allied forces reached the Han River without firing a single shot and regained possession of Inchon. On March 15, 1951, they recaptured Seoul.

When George heard the news, he immediately began making plans to return to the north showing the same confidence he'd demonstrated while organizing the hospital staff's retreat to the south. Records show that Doctor Rue personally helped almost 1,100 people leave Seoul for Pusan. Only five died along the way while many others remained missing. Considering the large number of people involved and the extreme difficulties of travel, it's considered a miracle that such a small number were injured or killed. None of the hospital staff died in the evacuation, and fewer than fifty Seventh-day Adventists throughout the entire country lost their lives during the war.

On Tuesday, March 20, 1951, George accompanied several American embassy personnel to the capital to inspect the hospital and college. What he found nearly broke his heart.

Rebuilding a Shattered Dream

George stared out the window of the automobile as it slowly made its way across the pontoon bridge spanning the Han River. He'd traveled north from Pusan with several American embassy personnel to inspect the war damage and was eager to determine the condition of the hospital and college grounds.

The streets of Seoul showed little activity. The only people he observed stumbling among the rubble were the very young and very old. All other former residents, both men and women between the ages of fifteen and thirty-five, had been displaced, captured, or killed. The city lay virtually flattened except for a few large buildings with windows blown out.

When they arrived at the American embassy compound, the group climbed over a large pile of rubble to get inside. The ambassador's home had sustained two direct hits.

The railway station lay in ruins, the Union headquarters had suffered extensive damage, and the Church-run press, which had, just months before, been heralding the good news of salvation, had been stripped. Only the time clock remained, forlornly waiting for someone to check in. But there were no workers and no one to read the results of their labors.

The city's water supply had been severely damaged. No electric current coursed through the wires laying twisted and burned across the streets. Food supplies didn't exist, and land mines bordered the main roads.

The hospital and school had suffered severe damage and loss. While the medical center itself still stood, the nurses' dormitory and one of the doctors' homes had been completely destroyed. Only chimneys remained, standing over the burned-out rubble like tattered vultures, offering mute testimony to the violence that had swept across the campus. Bullets and shrapnel had torn into all the other homes and buildings. Everything had been ransacked, leaving no medicines, linens, blankets, pillows, or mattresses.

Amazingly, George found the large X-ray machine, surgery table, and main sterilizer intact. Dental chairs, cabinets, and smaller X-ray machines also remained. The two large generators stood where he'd left them with only their magnetos removed. Many of the hospital beds, tables, chairs, and refrigerators had been taken.

George walked into the boiler room, and his heart sank. In the excitement of leaving, the man he had instructed to drain the system hadn't done his job. Frozen pipes had burst, causing extensive water damage throughout the structure.

In the distance, Doctor Rue could hear large-bore artillery pieces firing, reminding him that, while the fighting had moved north, the war was far from over. Explosions shook the windowpanes that remained.

Under the circumstances, George determined that he must postpone the reopening of the institution. As he made the long, arduous journey back to Pusan, his heart was heavy with grief but filled with determination. When possible, he'd return to Seoul with an army of his own made up of technicians, builders, and medical personnel. For now, the work on Cheju Island and in the city of Pusan needed his full attention.

During the first few months of operation, those two medical clinics had treated patients who were unable to pay. But the number of paying patients was rising quickly, especially in Pusan, enabling the hardworking doctors, nurses, and staff members to expand their services with additional equipment and supplies.

There was another reason George wanted to make sure that the medical programs on the island and in the southern city were earning their keep. When Seoul reopened, he'd need income to pay his staff and repair the war damage. While he knew the Adventist Church would provide as much as possible, and fellow Church members around the world would offer financial assistance as well, bringing the hospital back to full operation would take a lot of money. A *lot* of money.

Only four months later, in July 1951, George and his team of Adventist workers swung open the doors of the Seoul Sanitarium and Hospital. In doing so, they announced to the entire country that, while the Communists had destroyed the city and many of the buildings on the hospital campus, the enemy had failed to destroy what was most important—their Christian spirit.

For two years, George and Grace divided their time between Seoul and Pusan, each taking up posts at different ends of the country. Every couple of weeks, George would board the night train for the twelve-hour trip to Seoul to see special patients. He'd then board a southbound train the very next night for the return trip, falling asleep in the swaying passenger car as it clattered through the dark countryside. He'd arrive in Pusan in the morning, ready and eager to continue his work.

As expected, the Church they served came through. The Far Eastern Division of Seventh-day Adventists appropriated $20,000 for the new Seoul Sanitarium and Hospital. Congregations in North America added $100,000 gathered in just one countrywide offering!

The United States government furnished trucks, cement mixers, gravel, sand, and a host of other construction materials as well as additional funding. Even the beleaguered people of Korea did their part. A Christmas offering taken up in December brought in an amazing $15,000 to help keep the medical work alive and growing. Soon, more missionaries arrived to staff the hospital, school, and Church headquarters.

However, the rebuilding process was proving to be a challenge of enormous proportions. William H. Bergherm, secretary of the General Conference International Commission of the Medical Cadet Service, visited Seoul in February 1952 and then shared his experience with his church family in *The Review and Herald*. "How this hospital can take care of its 250 patients in the cold is more than I'm able to figure out," he wrote. "Where all [of these patients] are put is another mystery. Two and three in a small bed is the only solution so far. Mrs. Rue has a precious little [American/Korean] half-caste in a crib in the office beside the telephone. Poor thing! It was more dead than alive when it was first brought in. But love and good nursing are making a beautiful baby, the favorite of everyone."

On March 21 and 22, 1952, George, Grace, Miss Robson, and church members from throughout the area stood with tears in their eyes as two classes of nursing students, 1950 and 1952, did something that the war had postponed. They walked down the aisle in the first commencement ceremony at Seoul Sanitarium and Hospital in eleven years. Verna Pak led fifteen fellow classmates to the front of the chapel and, with gratitude filling her heart, received her diploma.

The number of graduates would have been larger, but the war had taken its toll. Some nursing students had been captured, some killed. Others had dropped out of the program. But, like the apostle Paul, the sixteen women standing before friends and family that day had fought the good fight of faith and, at long last, had finished the race.

As the war continued to rage to the north, sometimes within twenty miles of the campus, the medical team kept up their own relentless battle against illness and injury. Writing to friends that winter, George reported, "Communist guerrillas are getting bolder all the time. It's unsafe to travel the roads at night unless in a convoy. Trains have been fired on and dynamited. We'd like to know just how the peace talks will come out and when this war will end. Some days the outlook appears brighter than others. There is a question in the minds of many whether the cease-fire talks will result in anything of a permanent nature even if they do bring about a cease fire."

The hospital brimmed with patients, but only a handful could afford to pay for services received. The generosity of Church members worldwide and the additional funds donated by various government entities kept the doors open and the doctors and nurses on the job. Even in the face of such hardship and financial shortfalls, the facility stubbornly maintained its mission to heal the wounds of a nation.

During this time, there was another mission very close to Grace's heart, an outreach program that occupied center stage in her affections as the horrible war ground toward its inevitable conclusion. This mission focused on hands too young to fight and eyes too filled with pain to ignore.

Amazing Grace

Dr. Ernest Zinke, Jr., staff medical officer aboard the USS *Mount McKinley,* the flagship of the U. S. amphibious forces in the Pacific, stood looking at a little boy wearing a ragged, cut-down army uniform and muddy smile.

"That's exactly how we found him," a sailor said as he and his buddies crowded around the new arrival. "He just stepped out of his tiny homeless shelter, you know, those boxes built on posts along the main streets of Pusan, and said to us, 'Sirs, I'm hungry.' Took us by surprise. We . . . we couldn't just leave him there. We had to do something."

Ernest glanced out across the harbor at the morning sun that was just beginning to peek above the watery horizon. "The little guy saluted us and everything," the sailors pressed. "How could we leave him all alone on the street? Wouldn't be right."

"There are a lot of orphans wandering around these days," Ernest stated.

"Yes," responded the sailors, "but how many are wearing 'government issue'?"

The medical officer shook his head. "We can't keep a six-year-old boy on board this ship. It's against regulations."

"You're right, sir," the men chorused.

"But, you see, we figure an army unit was looking after him before," one of the seamen pointed out, ruffling the boy's dark, uncombed hair with his fingers. "Then they must have shipped out. Now he's got no one. Come on, doc, he won't eat much. Me and my buddies will take really good care of Jimmy. We promise."

"Jimmy?"

"Yeah, we kind of gave him a name. We know it's not Korean, but since he's wearing an American uniform and all, we figured he could use a good American name."

Ernest bent low and looked into the bright brown eyes of the unexpected visitor. The boy's smile broadened as he lifted his dirt-stained right hand to his forehead and issued a smart, but tired, salute. "Sir, I'm hungry," he stated.

The medical officer shook his head and sighed. "Just keep him out of the way," he ordered. "And . . . and get Jimmy something to eat. Oh, and give him a bath, too. Use lots of soap."

The crew kept their newfound friend for several weeks, even when they sailed around the southern tip of Korea from Pusan and traveled north to Inchon harbor. The lad became popular with everyone on board, up to the highest-ranking officer. At night when the sailors crowded into the recreation room to watch movies, Jimmy was always first to announce, "Attention on deck!" when the admiral arrived. Then he'd climb up onto the officer's lap and would be fast asleep before the last scene faded from the screen.

Various crewmen were assigned to watch him and try to keep him out of danger, which proved next to impossible on a working ship at war. Several times, the little deckhand almost fell overboard. Without the quick intervention of someone walking by, he would have electrocuted himself while digging around in the ship's electronic equipment. Then, one day, Jimmy disappeared. After a frantic search, crewmembers found him in the engine room admiring the roaring, spinning, diesel-driven crankshaft—a highly dangerous area even for grown men.

Everyone agreed that Jimmy needed a new home; somewhere he could be safe and, hopefully, surrounded by children his own age. But where? Korea was in the throes of a violent war. Thousands of homeless children roamed the rubble-strewn streets in every devastated town and city, searching for food and shelter. They couldn't just drop him off at the next port and wish him luck. He'd die, and they knew it.

"I've heard about a place," Ernest announced as he and a group of fellow sailors gathered for an informal meeting on the subject. "You see, I'm a graduate of the College of Medical Evangelists in Loma Linda, California. Another doctor who took his training there, a George Rue, is in Seoul with his wife, Grace. They operate a hospital, and, if I've got my information straight, they run an orphanage too. Why don't we check it out? At least Jimmy would be around good medical care if he ever needed it."

Everyone wholeheartedly agreed that Ernest might be onto something.

It just so happened that the *Mount McKinley* was about to dock in the harbor at Inchon. As soon as he could arrange time ashore, Dr. Zinke acquired a jeep, a Marine driver, and some groceries. He asked Don Seaman, a line officer from the ship, to accompany him and Jimmy for a quick visit to Seoul.

Arriving at the hospital, they found Grace at her desk in the basement of the building, hard at work, surrounded by a miniature army of Korean boys and girls. "Mrs. Rue," Ernest called out. "I'm Dr. Zinke, and this is my friend Don Seaman. We're from the *Mount McKinley* and have a bit of a dilemma. You see we found this little boy on the streets of Pusan and ..."

"Doctor," Grace interrupted, "we've got three hundred and twenty orphans under our care right now." The men saw a smile creep across her face. "I guess three hundred and twenty-one won't make that much difference."

Ernest extended his hand. "Mrs. Rue, you are truly an angel of mercy here in Korea. But, I want you to know that we haven't shown up empty-handed. Jimmy comes with his own groceries!"

"Now that's good news," Grace laughed. "Come on, I'll show you gentlemen to our storeroom."

When Ernest and Don walked into the storage area, their hearts sank. There was so little of anything, yet three hundred and twenty-one boys and girls were depending on the hospital to keep them alive. Seeing their faces, Grace interjected with firm conviction, "I've never had to put a child to bed hungry yet."

Her spirit impressed the visitors, especially Don.

A month or so later, a big box addressed to "Amphibious Forces Pacific" and labeled "High Priority" arrived on board the *Mount McKinley*. The admiral's staff opened it and found that it was filled with food concentrates, vitamins, and other supplies. The officer in charge chuckled. "Looks like the work of our own Don Seaman."

"I thought he was sailing a desk at Navy intelligence in Washington D.C.," Ernest said, inspecting the supplies.

"He is," his companion stated. "But he's still fighting the Korean War the only way he can."

Ernest procured another jeep and driver and headed ashore with the big box strapped to the back of the vehicle. But, the journey to Grace's orphanage did not proceed as planned. A few miles down the road, they came to a barrier thrown up by Korean customs officials.

"What's in the box?" the men asked, eyeing the load suspiciously.

"Supplies for an orphanage," Ernest declared. "A gift from a Navy man in Washington, D.C."

"You can't take this box into the city without paying duty on the contents."

"Duty? These are supplies for a bunch of hungry kids! Can't you let this one go through?"

"No, you must pay."

With a heavy heart, Ernest and his driver headed back toward the ship. On the way, they passed a security post set up by marines patrolling the area. After hearing their story, a second jeep suddenly appeared filled with some very large and very heavily armed marines. "Follow us," they commanded.

As the tiny convoy approached the customs roadblock, the marines fingered their weapons and announced to the agent, "The jeep behind us is going through, so open the gate *right now!*" There was no further argument.

Grace was overjoyed when she saw the contents of the box. "You and your friends have been so supportive," she said fighting back tears. "I just want you to know how much we appreciate your thoughtfulness."

Once the supplies had been unloaded and placed in the storage room, she invited Ernest and his driver to a spot by a playground where dozens of children ran about with flushed cheeks amid happy laughter. "You see that little guy over there?" she asked, pointing in the direction of a nurse holding a small child in her arms. "Some women appeared at our doorstep earlier this year, held up that baby and said, 'Send to father's country.' Then they left."

"Father's country?" Ernest asked. "What did she mean?"

Grace sighed. "One of the tragedies of this Korean War is the large number of abandoned and orphaned children who roam the countryside. Many of them are half American, half Korean. The nationals here consider those kids to be 'half-breeds,' or nonpersons. They suffer terrible discrimination and are often left to survive on their own. They have a name for them. *Toogees.* I'm afraid some are even killed.

"Then we had one boy brought to us with a broken jaw. He had been that way for several weeks. His little face was swollen to twice its normal size, and he was in severe pain. But you know what? He never complained. Not once. He let us fix his jaw without uttering a single word.

"Many of our kids suffer from tuberculosis, worms, and lice. Some are only days old when they're abandoned down at the gatehouse or in the hospital waiting room. After they're well, no one comes for them. We've had servicemen find children in culverts along the roadside or in burned-out buildings, just waiting to die. It's enough to break your heart."

Among the playing children, Ernest recognized Jimmy, his smile radiant, his laughter filled with newfound hope and joy.

"We're providing some schooling and, hopefully, teaching these kids how to earn a living after the war ends," Grace continued. "But, what's most important, we're bringing them up in a Christian atmosphere. They're learning about Jesus and know that there's a new world waiting for them where it doesn't matter who their earthly parents are because, in heaven, they'll all have the same Father."

Ernest returned to the *Mount McKinley,* his heart bursting with gratitude for the work his new American friends were doing within the war-torn country. He knew that they were medical missionaries in the truest sense of the word.

Late one afternoon, a Korean mother arrived at the Seoul Sanitarium and Hospital with her four children in tow, ranging from ages three to thirteen. Their home had been destroyed just behind the front lines forty miles to the northeast. A large shell had instantly killed her husband and an older daughter.

When the mother stumbled onto the campus, she was seriously ill. The entire group was badly undernourished, dirty, weak, and tired from their forty-mile trek.

Hospital personnel bathed and fed each member of the family, and the sick mother was immediately hospitalized. The next morning, she died, leaving her children to become the newest residents at the orphanage.

During the war, civilians tried their best to keep out of harm's way. But, in the intense confusion of battle, families became separated, and children found themselves alone and lost. Many times, entire families vanished in the flash of fire and smoke created by an exploding shell, bomb, or land mine.

Grace Rue holds two of "her children."

Thousands of young boys and girls became maimed or fell victim to exposure and starvation. Some could recall vivid images of watching their parents die.

Week after week, malnourished and exhausted groups of adults and children showed up at the orphanage door. The adults would plead with Grace to accept the children, explaining that they'd traveled great distances and were unable to find food. "Of course I'll take them," Grace would respond with unwavering kindness and understanding.

One day four adults approached the orphanage; Grace recognized them as parents who, years before, had left their children in her care. "Do you still have them?" they asked timidly.

"Yes, I do," Grace responded.

"Please, may we have them back?"

"Of course. I'll go get them."

The family could hardly believe their ears. In their minds, they'd given their children away and didn't have the right to see them again. But as their now smiling and well-nourished sons and daughters came out to greet them, they found themselves enveloped with arms they thought had been removed from their lives forever. The reunion brought tears to every eye that witnessed it.

At the end of July 1952, Grace moved her growing orphanage to eight acres of land about a mile and a half from the hospital. Her family of children eventually topped 580 boys and girls ranging in age from a few days to seventeen years. The Rues proudly named their new project "The Seoul Sanitarium and Hospital Orphanage," hired a full-time manager, and set to work repairing and cleaning an existing brick building sitting on the property. With the help of the children, they dug a well eight feet across and thirty feet deep. A little rail car hauled dirt from the site.

As the Rues worked to maintain their orphanage and keep the medical work going at hospitals in Seoul and Pusan, the war continued to rage to the north. Among those involved in the conflict were Seventh-day Adventist servicemen, most of them belonging to Eighth Army medical battalions. Their assignment was to treat and transfer wounded Allied forces by jeep ambulance from forward positions to the many Mobile Army Surgical Hospital (M.A.S.H.) units scattered back of the front lines. Often these American GIs would travel down to Seoul and show up at the hospital looking for comfort and some good American home cooking. George and Grace gladly accepted them into their home for Sabbath dinner, serving them cafeteria style, and listening to their stories. During the height of the fighting, 75 to 150 servicemen showed up each week! One memorable Sabbath saw 300 war-weary soldiers on campus.

In early spring 1953, General Maxwell D. Taylor, commander of the Eighth Army, arranged for Dr. E. N. Dick of the General Conference War Service Commission to spend three days on the front lines. On the weekend of March 7, every Seventh-day Adventist soldier was given leave by the high command to meet with Dr. Dick at the Seoul Sanitarium and Hospital. One young man quipped with a happy smile, "This is the first time I was ever ordered to go to church!"

Around three o'clock on Friday afternoon, military vehicles—everything from six-wheeled transports to ambulances and small pickups—began arriving on the sanitarium grounds. Some soldiers came clad in dress uniform with polished shoes. Others arrived directly from the front lines dressed in Army fatigues, helmets, and rubber footwear often stained with blood.

Dr. Dick led the soldiers in the ordinances of humility ceremony. Soldier knelt before soldier, washing each other's feet in water held within their helmets. A genuine spirit of brotherly love pervaded the deeply moving service. One hundred and twenty-six men participated.

Afterward, the cheerful soldiers enjoyed a much-appreciated meal prepared by the ever-busy hands of Grace Rue and Miss Robson.

The next day, the visitors were back at the front, putting their lives on the line to save their fallen comrades.

In the summer of 1953, a long-anticipated armistice was signed in Panmunjom. Chaplain Carl R. Holden, an Adventist with the 44th M.A.S.H. division, headed for the front lines smoldering thirty-five miles away. Writing for *The Review and Herald* in August of that year, he shared how it looked and sounded when the deadly conflict finally ground to a halt.

"July 27, 1953. With the cease-fire deadline just an hour and a half off, there seems to be little slackening in the number of artillery rounds going out.

"Now it's 9:15 P.M. Just forty-five minutes remain. From this point on our line I see the characteristic white flashes of our Willie Peters (white phosphorus) artillery shells bursting on enemy positions just 3,300 yards in front of us. Other artillery shells whistle over our heads, headed for enemy fortifications farther north.

"Twenty minutes before deadline. Artillery is starting to quiet down now. However, to our left flank, I hear sporadic bursts of machine-gun fire.

"Now it's exactly 10 P.M. All is quiet on the Korean battlefront. Fellow believers, will you pray with me that this quietness and peace may continue in this land so torn by war?"

Following the signing of the armistice, patronage of the Seoul Sanitarium and Hospital continued to increase, soon almost reaching pre-war numbers. Patients filled every bed, and beds lined the hallways.

Before Doctor Rue left Korea in 1954 for a long-delayed furlough in the United States, the nation honored him at a historic presidential party. Surrounded by Korea's most notable politicians, educators, physicians, and businessmen, President Rhee placed a medallion around his friend's neck. "This is the Republic of Korea Medal," the president announced, "the highest civilian honor our nation can bestow for devoted service to the people of Korea." Many in the wildly cheering audience had experienced Doctor Rue's care and medical expertise firsthand.

The United States armed forces as well as the United Nations also praised George's work as the smoke cleared and people of Korea began the long process of rebuilding their shattered lives.

The country lay in ruins. The United States sustained 157, 530 causalities with 33,629 dead. South Korean losses were placed at 1,312,837 military casualties and 415,004 dead. Britain, Australia, and Turkey gave up 16,532 of their countrymen to injury or death.

On the Communist side, the numbers were staggering with estimates reaching well over two million.

In 1955, fresh from America and with pockets full of funds from the United Nations Reconstruction Agency, the Adventist Church, and dedicated individuals from around the world, Doctor Rue purchased a plot of land in Pusan and built a thirty-bed hospital. The "Old Barn" went back to being what it was designed to be.

Grace found herself leading a charge against child homelessness that would eventually reach around the world.

Mother of
Many

As war clouds lifted over the burned and broken land of South Korea, George and Grace found themselves facing an almost impossible task—to help rebuild the lives of thousands whose minds and bodies had been devastated by the violent hostilities of the past three years. While George concentrated mostly on the medical work, Grace turned her attention to the orphanage. But, she didn't have to carry the burden alone.

Commander Zinke, the Adventist Navy doctor who had arranged for "Jimmy McKinley's" care, accepted the responsibility of spreading the news about the orphanage to his friends and colleagues in America.

Ed Neuman from Pomona, California, one of Grace's former classmates, collected free samples of vitamins and baby foods from physicians' offices.

Southern California representatives of Mead Johnson and Company donated considerable quantities of their products.

Various churches, service clubs, and Scout troops collected food and clothing and shipped them to the Seoul Sanitarium and Hospital Orphanage in a military convoy made up of six large, ten-wheeled Army trucks. Six boxes that missed connections for the shipment were airlifted across the Pacific. Grace wrote of her gratitude, explaining that the vitamins and baby foods had actually saved lives.

Commander Zinke then organized an ongoing program to provide a constant stream of relief packages through the United States Naval Amphibious Base at Coronado, California. The greatest needs, according to Dr. Zinke, were infant and dried foods, warm clothing, bedding, vitamin preparation, and pharmaceuticals. Antibiotics topped the list.

In 1954 the Seventh-day Adventist Church collected hundreds of boxes of clothing and thousands of pounds of rice for distribution in Korea.

On a thirty-six-acre camp-meeting site in Lynwood, California, sixty-five Dorcas Society clubs gathered to create what the press called "the nation's biggest baby shower." Five thousand members put their 50,000 fingers to work, sewing baby garments for the orphans of Korea.

In time, the Rues received so much support that they were able to share some of their rich bounty with an American Indian school back in the western United States.

The orphanage's greatest expenses centered on food and educational supplies, a need that caught the attention of the United States Army 326th Communication Reconnaissance Company located near Seoul. Members willingly aided the Rues in fund raising by sending more than 500 letters to people in the United States, requesting paper, pencils, books, and crayons. They solicited clothing in anticipation of the coming winter and asked for powdered food of all kinds to supplement the rice rations received from the United Nations Civil Assistance Command. Cold hard cash was on their "needs" list as well, and they raised funds to purchase school desks, locally printed books, and other supplies. A few of the men came each week to teach English to the older children.

Friends in Australia shipped seventeen bales of clothing. The Girl Scouts of America packed forty drums of clothing and supplies—items they'd collected throughout local neighborhoods.

Back in Korea, children arriving at the orphanage quickly found that, mixed in with copious amounts of love and attention, was a new structure and purpose for their lives.

Their day began at 6:00 A.M. when they rose, dressed, and cleaned their rooms. Morning worship started at 6:30 sharp. Breakfast warmed

Children play at the main gate of the "old" orphanage building.

their tummies at 7:00, and school classes took their full attention from 8:00 to noon.

After lunch, the children reported to their jobs on the farm, in the garden, or at the laundry. The orphanage farm did well, rewarding young laborers with abundant harvests of rice, sweet potatoes, and soybeans. The orphans also cared for animals including rabbits, a puppy, and about 200 chickens.

In the winter they constructed homemade ice sleds by attaching skate runners to wooden platforms. Kids also pushed one another over the ice in old shipping crates.

After supper at 5:00 P.M., it was time for play, followed by evening worship and study. The scheduled environment, with days filled with a variety of activities, provided a welcome sense of organization and security.

Kimchi making became an annual event. Hundreds of gallons of the spicy food were prepared and buried for the coming year. To the outsider, the preparation of this oriental staple doesn't make much sense. But to the Koreans, there's nothing better than a hearty serving of kimchi during cold winter months.

Kimchi is similar to sauerkraut. Chinese cabbage, white radishes, and chopped pears are combined with copious amounts of cayenne pepper. The mixture is placed in clay pots or urns holding approximately thirty gallons each, and then each pot is filled with salt water. A hole is dug, and the covered containers are buried in the ground topped with a foot or so of straw. During the winter, kimchi is removed from its earthen storage bin and greatly enjoyed—in spite of its strong and enduring odor—with a side dish of rice or vegetables.

The children line up for inspection.

The program at the orphanage was so successful that nearby residents asked whether they could send their children to school there too. But, most of the time, space limitations prevented attendance from village boys and girls. In some cases, they were allowed to attend because there were no other schools available. But the orphanage's children were always free to invite their village friends to join them for church services twice a week. Everyone had a great time.

As their "family" increased in size, but the number of available beds didn't, the Rues found they had to sleep kids two to a mattress, one at each end. They double-decked some of the beds, placing two kids in each, with the younger ones on the lower deck. For very small babies, George and Grace divided regular hospital beds into three compartments, lovingly placing two infants in each.

Laughing, wiggling, adoring children surrounded Grace whenever she arrived at the orphanage. She'd kneel down and give them all the love she could. Every boy and girl claimed her as their "mother," a title she relished. "Just let the children crawl all over me," she'd often say when staff members tried to constrain the excited little ones.

One day a family left a baby girl on the doorstep of Grace's housekeeper. Eventually, they discovered that the infant was an identical twin and that the family had decided they simply didn't need an extra girl. In some societies, such a decision would be considered callous or cold. In post-war Korea, it was often the result of painful necessity.

During a furlough to the United States, the Rues gave mission talks at various churches. At one, they happened to mention that Koreans really enjoy music. "We'd love to start an orchestra at the orphanage," they told the gathering. "Our manager's daughter is giving piano lessons, but we'd like to offer more. An orchestra would do nicely!"

The audience responded. When George and Grace returned to Korea, they brought with them a box filled with a dozen musical instruments. Immediately, the orphanage formed an orchestra, and the children loved it!

Butch, a fourteen-year-old with a quick smile and a patient, pleasant disposition, became one of its first members. Because polio had claimed his legs, leaving him paralyzed from the waist down, other children had to carry him from place to place. But he never complained. He always appeared smiling and happy, eager to play his part with unrestrained enthusiasm.

The orphanage orchestra performed at Doctor Rue's "Hwan-gap," his sixtieth birthday celebration, held in 1959 in the beautiful garden in front of the hospital. George didn't want anyone to make a big deal out of his turning a year older. But, because he was so well-respected, a party was planned in spite of his protests. More than a thousand employees, families, villagers, and patients showed up for the celebration.

When the much loved and admired Miss Robson, the hospital's director of nurses, adopted a Korean daughter and took her on a visit to

the United States, the story made front-page news from Seattle to San Diego. "Patricia Lea is one of hundreds of war babies whose fathers are unknown American GIs," the *Los Angeles Times* stated in its December 21, 1953 issue. "These children are unaccepted by Koreans and unwanted by their American fathers." In the interview that followed, Miss Robson reported that the Adventist-run orphanage was vital because there was no place for these children in Korea. "The

A Korean orphan boy enjoys a bowl of rice.

people there feel they don't belong," she said. "One little girl even has blond hair and freckles."

Within two weeks of that news report, the orphanage received 608 letters and telegrams requesting to adopt a child. Between 1954 and 1957, the institution placed 122 orphans with moms and dads in the United States. During that same time, Korean families adopted more than seventy children. Others experienced the unspeakable joy of being claimed by relatives.

One little boy, on his way to America, started telling people about his new family. "See," he said, pointing at pictures he held tightly in his chubby hands. "This is my new mother, father, and big brother."

When the adoptive family met him for the first time in a room provided by the airport, his new brother handed him one of two little toy trucks. Both boys immediately dropped to their knees and began playing as if they'd been brothers for years.

Grace and her orphanage took an active approach in preparing children for the future. Although some such facilities released their charges at eighteen years of age, the Rues felt that a young person of that age is not yet ready to find his or her place in society alone. Because work was scarce, many Korean young people were forced to turn to begging or stealing in order to stay alive. So the children in the Rues' orphanage received help until they had completed their education or learned a trade.

By 1960, some of the boys and girls had matured into fine young men and women. Twenty-five were already enrolled at the academy, and twenty more were ready to begin classes. Of those attending college, two requested ministerial training, one studied to be a pharmacist, and four enrolled in the nurses course. Two boys planned to follow in George's footsteps. They wanted to become physicians.

Foster parents who financially supported specific children from afar, were encouraged to write and send photos. "You don't realize how much your letters mean to them," Grace would write. "It gives them the thing they need so much; a feeling of not being alone. They know they have a family who cares for them. It's a real morale builder."

Each year, the Rues sent Christmas letters to family and friends. In 1964, Grace included a poignant story. "A little fellow," she wrote, "after being with his new parents for a couple of days, returned with them to the orphanage for a visit. One of his former playmates came up and started to take hold of the mother's hand. The little boy resented this immediately and let it be known that this was *his* mother and that he was not sharing her with anyone!"

The Rues' 1965 Christmas message provided readers with an insight into the impact the orphanage was having. "Our family now consists of 235 children. Of these, twenty-one reside in the dormitory at the Korean Union College, eight will graduate this December from the Home Economics course, thirty-four are attending our high school, and seventeen of those will graduate in February. Most want to go on to college. Twenty-three children are in our middle school at the orphanage, and forty-eight attend the primary school. Four girls are in the nursing course.

"Our boy who graduated last year from the nursing course is taking a two-year course in physiotherapy. This is something we need in the hospital and trust that he will be a real help to us. One boy who has returned from [his term of duty in] the Korean Army is going ahead with dental school, working part-time at the hospital to help on his expenses. One girl is attending a school for the blind, and one is attending a school for the deaf. Twelve children have been sent to the U.S., and twenty-four to Norway for adoption during the year.

"One of the older orphan boys walked for three miles to conduct two branch Sabbath Schools in a Korean home. Up to fifteen adults and between twenty and thirty children attended his meetings. During the Week of Prayer that followed, he arose at 3:00 A.M. to walk there in time for the early services. Koreans prefer early services.

"Every year the orphanage conducts Vacation Bible Schools in the surrounding countryside. Forty-five children were baptized following one effort. Last year twenty-five of the older orphans spent most of their summer vacations conducting meetings for children in the mornings, visiting homes in the afternoons, and holding meetings as late as 9:00 P.M. to accommodate adults after they returned home from working in the fields. One boy had an audience of 400 adults."

Grace Rue took great pains to find the best homes she possibly could for all she called "my children." About 350 went to the United States. Another 200 went to Norway and Sweden. She arranged for travel visas, and various airlines provided special accommodations for the escorts.

Jimmy McKinley, the little boy who'd won the hearts of an entire shipload of sailors, found a new home with a Seventh-day Adventist couple in America.

No matter where her children went, Grace or another missionary would accompany them to meet their new families. Some overseas parents came to Korea to welcome new children into their home.

Grace kept careful records to see how her boys and girls were doing after they left Korea. She thrilled at news that her children were well and happy in their new lives.

At long last, after decades of service to the people of Korea, George and Grace made plans to return to the United States permanently. Some of the officers at the Far Eastern Division and the General Conference of Seventh-day Adventists discussed with Grace the possibility of closing the orphanage. "No," she responded emphatically. "These children have been raised with Seventh-day Adventist ideals and training. To place them in homes that would not honor their background would be traumatic for them. I'm not about to let my children be moved from the only home they have ever known."

Her strong words carried with them the painful sting of experience. She'd faced a difficult situation after placing a child in the non-Adventist home of an American Army officer in Korea. The boy found it difficult to adjust.

To honor her respectful, but emphatic, demand, another woman was found to take Grace's place. Fay Welter, later writing in her book, *Diary of a New Mother*, wrote, "July. Arrived in Korea and am now the mother of 200-plus children ranging in age from a few days old to their middle twenties. What a family, and I am not even married!

"August. Mrs. Rue is leaving, and I am soon going to be at the helm all by myself. My knees are smiting one against the other.

"November. For the first time I had the joy of presenting two babies to their adoptive parents. What beautiful expressions shone on the faces of those parents as they tenderly took my Korean dolls in their arms for the first time. Adoptions are fun!"

The Seoul Sanitarium and Hospital Orphanage eventually cared for more than 1,000 children. It finally ceased operation in the mid-1970s.

All the boys and girls and young men and women who spent part of their lives within its safe and loving embrace gained a deep, abiding understanding of their heavenly Father. In the aftermath of a violent, horrible war, it stood among the hills at the edge of a devastated city, offering a bright, new future while helping children learn to cope with the agonies of the past.

Grace's orphanage, like her husband's hospitals and clinics, was far more than a place where broken bodies and shattered hearts came to heal. In the company of these two incredible individuals, the people of Korea found hope waiting in the darkness and learned of the existence of a glorious, everlasting tomorrow.

Final
Service

Doctor Rue, at age sixty-eight, retired with a hero's farewell on July 1, 1967. Everyone agreed he deserved a break after thirty-five years of medical service to Korea.

George had given up a lucrative family practice in the United States to spend most of his medical/surgical career in a land far beyond his homeland's horizon. The most he ever earned was a little more than $600 per month, and that was at the *end* of his career in Korea.

He'd been a boss, mentor, and friend to thousands and had always led by example. If something needed to be done, he didn't look for someone else to do it. He just rolled up his sleeves and got busy.

Years earlier, Walter E. Macpherson, MD, had written an editorial in the November 1954 edition of *The Medical Evangelist.* "Unselfish service of superior quality is the highest attainment in life," he'd stated. "For one to give this service where the needs are the greatest is an indication of his character and of his objectives. To produce individuals with such attitudes and qualities is the primary purpose of the College of Medical Evangelists."

With his life, George had hung flesh and blood on the CME principles he'd learned during his medical education at Loma Linda.

Dr. and Mrs. Rue are surrounded by nurses at Dr. Rue's 60th birthday celebration, 1959.

Duane Johnson of the General Conference penned his thoughts in a letter of commendation dated April 24, 1967.

"Within a few days you will be leaving Korea, and while this will be difficult for you, I can assure you that your friends here are anticipating your arrival. While welcoming you back to the homeland, I want to pass along from the General Conference Committee the deep appreciation our church people and the General Conference have for the many years of dedicated service you have given as a medical missionary worker since 1929. We have recorded in our minutes a statement giving some detail regarding this service, and we want to pass along the affection and commendation of the brethren.

"The service you have given and the experience you and Mrs. Rue have had will be an inspiration and help to our people. After you have had a little period to visit your relatives and friends, we shall probably be coming to you with a request to help inspire the youth in our schools and churches to serve overseas in various ways. Our evangelism in this country will also be strengthened if your experience and your living faith can be shared with others through radio and TV and newspaper reports. Our people in the churches and our conference workers will be looking to you for assistance in these various ways."

The Joon Ang University in Seoul awarded Doctor Rue an honorary Doctor of Laws degree for his work in both Seoul and Pusan during the Korean War. From the Su Do Medical School, George received an honorary doctor's degree, a very high honor for a foreigner.

Just before he left the country, George gave the hospital his shares in a Korean pharmaceutical company. Within ten years after his departure, his small $2,100 investment was valued at nearly $65,000.

Both George and Grace agreed that the greatest reward of their lives was the satisfaction of knowing that they had faithfully followed in the footsteps of the Great Physician. Quoted in the *Far Eastern Division Outlook* in July 1967, Doctor Rue stated, "I have dedicated my life to the people of Korea. Healing the sick and caring for those who are less fortunate is part of the gospel. As a Christian, it is my duty to follow the example of Christ who was also a missionary."

Dr. George and Mrs. Grace Rue, 1960.

The Rues retired to Marrowstone Island, forty miles north of Seattle, to a simple home built by their son-in-law, Leland Mitchell. George took up residence in his favorite swivel chair where he could watch television or, with a gentle push with his heel, turn to watch the boats passing between Marrowstone and Whidbey Islands. But Korea still tugged at their hearts. During their retirement years, they returned to Korea six times to work as replacements for vacationing hospital staff. The facility would fill to overflowing whenever he walked the corridors.

While his leaving marked the close of an important and selfless career in Adventist health care, it also marked the beginning of a new era for Korea. Soon after George's departure, construction began on a brand-new hospital just behind the old one. It opened its doors on July 16, 1976, offering 160 beds and thirty bassinets. George, standing proudly with the assembled guests, welcomed Francesca Rhee, the widow of the former president, to the celebration.

In a September letter written to Duane Johnson in 1979, George spoke of his final trip to Korea and how the large hospital debt had been paid off in full. As usual, the facility was full to overflowing. "Some have to be turned away for lack of beds," he reported. "We see approximately 1,000 patients each Sunday."

Today, the Seoul Adventist Hospital has grown to 406 beds. The Republic of Korea has emerged from almost total devastation to become a world-class economy. Seoul ranks as one of the ten largest cities in the world. It played host to the 1988 Summer Olympic Games and co-hosted (with Japan) the World Cup in 2002. Korea is growing and flourishing through high-technology industries, manufacturing, and tourism.

However, ongoing efforts to reunify North and South Korea have failed. Although the nation has been overpowered numerous times in its 5,000-year history, its courageous people have always maintained their own identity, traditions, and language. In spite of its tragic history, the proud little country anticipates a better tomorrow.

The demilitarized zone, running along the thirty-eighth parallel, filled with land mines and watched over by armed men peering through binoculars, still separates Korea's people. However, there's hope that, in time, the country can be reunified.

In 1982, the Loma Linda University School of Medicine Alumni Association named Doctor Rue "Alumnus of the Year." In announcing the award, Roger W. Barnes, MD, CME Class of 1922, stated, "The man who forgets himself in his zeal to help the poor, the sick, the destitute, and the helpless, is the one who merits honor.

Final Service

"Our Alumnus of the Year has not amassed a fortune, nor has he conquered a nation. He has done greater deeds than these. He has improved the lot of thousands of the poorest and most destitute human beings on earth. He has clothed and fed babies and children who were cold and hungry. He has relieved suffering. He has rebuilt broken bodies. He has saved hundreds of lives. He has given new hope and courage and spiritual inspiration to all with whom he has associated.

"Our Alumnus of the Year has never thought of obtaining honor nor of receiving acclaim; but honor and acclaim have been bestowed upon him even though he has tried to avoid them."

That same year, Grace became the fiftieth anniversary Woman of the Year. Recognition as one of the legendary women who displayed the Seventh-day Adventist missionary spirit so well for so many years surprised Grace. "I am deeply honored and very appreciative," she responded.

In his retirement, George never lost his interest in building boats. During his tenure overseas, when he'd return to Korea after various furloughs to America, he'd start building a new vessel to be completed by his next summer vacation. Then he and Grace would sail around the Korean islands only to sell the boat before heading to the United States five years later. Upon his return to Korea, he'd start building again. Altogether, Doctor Rue constructed six sailboats ranging from eighteen to twenty feet in length.

After moving to Marrowstone Island, he and Leland bought a surplus thirty-eight-foot powerboat from the United States Marines. Together the two families spent many happy days boating and camping among the islands around Puget Sound.

He also enjoyed listening to Grace play the piano. "I love to sit down and just make a noise on it," she told friends. "Even though George can't carry a tune, he loves my piano playing, no matter how terrible it is."

One chilly morning George looked out of his and Grace's bedroom window. "The old man is on his walk," he announced, pointing at an elderly neighbor who was ambling along the road, a routine he followed faithfully every day at this time. "But, wait, there's

125

something following him. I . . . I can't make out what it is."

George didn't like mysteries, especially when they paraded right by his window. A little later that day, he discovered what it was that had been escorting the gentleman on his walk. A houseguest who'd been staying with the couple stood at the front door with a tabby kitten held tightly in his outstretched hands. "Your neighbor called and asked me to hang onto this kitten," the visitor stated. "The man said that if it followed him home, his dog would kill it."

Thinking the situation was well in hand, George turned and walked to his favorite chair by the fireplace. No sooner had he sat down when, *plop,* he found the kitten in his lap. Apparently, the warm fire and gentle voice of the retired doctor proved too much of a temptation to the little animal. The kitten put its paws up on George's chest and licked his chin, sealing their friendship forever. Through the years, the animal spent much time curled up asleep on George's lap.

At long last, as the years slipped by, George's health began to fail. In time, he was confined to bed under a doctor's care. Grace tenderly watched over him in their cozy home on quiet Marrowstone Island.

On November 18, 1993, George awoke from a restless sleep. For weeks he hadn't been able to eat anything but spoonfuls of liquid nourishment. When he tried to swallow, he'd choke.

He grew weaker and weaker. In one last moment of intimacy, he reached for Grace and pursed his lips, indicating that he wanted a kiss. With tears flowing down her cheeks, Grace squeezed his hand and gently placed her lips on his. Then she prayed aloud, "Dear Lord. Please help George." She ended her supplication with, "And may we meet again in heaven."

George tried to speak, but couldn't. He relaxed with an expression of acceptance and closed his eyes, never to open them again.

Those eyes that had witnessed man's inhumanity to man, seen the sorrows of war, and observed evil as it violently strangled a nation, spent their last moments gazing into the face of his attentive, devoted, and loving helpmate. He breathed his last at 8:15 that evening. He was ninety-four.

Today, Grace lives alone, keeping her doors always open to the downtrodden and homeless.

Doctor George Henry Rue became a giant among men. He served anyone in need, from patients in run-down shacks, to Syngman Rhee at the presidential palace. Personnel from the United States embassy and the United Nations, as well as forgotten, unwanted children felt his healing touch. More than most, he understood the temporary nature of this earthly life.

George and Grace Rue, in closing one of their many letters to supporters, expressed the words they lived by. "We look forward to the soon return of Christ when He will take all who love Him home to heaven. What a grand reunion that will be! May we all be ready and waiting to meet Him."

If you enjoyed this book, you'll enjoy these as well:

Under the Shadow of the Rising Sun
Donald and Vesta West Mansell. A missionary family en route to Africa gets caught in the Japanese occupation of the Philippines and spends three years in a prisoner of war camp. A powerful true story of survival and faith during the Second World War.
0-8163-1976-6. Paperback.
US$14.99, Can$23.99.

Mission Pilot
Eileen Lantry. The true adventures of David Gates, a missionary pilot who repeatedly experienced the miracles of God in his life. Through hijackings, prison, and many other narrow escapes, David proves that living for God is still the highest adventure.
0-8163-1870-0. Paperback.
US$12.99, Can$20.99.

In His Hands
Sophie Berecz and Arpad Soo. The exciting true story of God's miraculous protection of a Romanian Adventist pastor who smuggled literature behind the iron curtain. Imprisonment, divorce, poverty and ultimately, financial blessings all play in part this amazing story.
0-8163-1903-0. Paperback.
US$12.99, Can$20.99.

Order from your ABC by calling **1-800-765-6955**, or get online and shop our virtual store at **www.adventistbookcenter.com**.
• Read a chapter from your favorite book
• Order online
• Sign up for email notices on new products

Prices subject to change without notice.